WORLD OF ANIMALS

WORLD OF ANIMALS

First published in 2008 by Miles Kelly Publishing Ltd
Bardfield Centre, Great Bardfield, Essex, CM7 4SL

The sections in this book are also available as individual titles

This edition printed in 2009

2 4 6 8 10 9 7 5 3

Editorial Director Belinda Gallagher
Art Director Jo Brewer
Assistant Editor Carly Blake
Designers Candice Bekir, Jo Brewer, Sally Lace, Simon Lee,
Louisa Leitao, Sophie Pelham, Elaine Wilkinson, Alix Wood
Production Manager Elizabeth Brunwin
Reprographics Stephan Davis, Ian Paulyn
Editions Manager Bethan Ellish

ISBN 978-1-84810-012-1

Printed in China

British Library Cataloguing-in-Publication Data
A catalogue record for this book is available from the British Library

ACKNOWLEDGEMENTS
All artworks are from the Miles Kelly Artwork Bank
Cover artwork: Mike Saunders

The publishers would like to thank the following
sources for the use of their photographs:

Page 38 Fred Bavendam/Minden Pictures/FLPA; 48 Michael Prince/Corbis; 50 Amos Nachoum/Corbis; 94 Grigory Kubatyan/Fotolia; 96 Photolibrary
Group Ltd; 100 Elenathewise/Fotolia; 102 David Hosking/FLPA; 103 Photolibrary Group Ltd; 105 Photolibrary Group Ltd; 106 Martin Will/Fotolia;
107 Andy Rouse/Corbis; 108 Gordan Court/Hedgehog House/Minden Pictures/FLPA; 109 Photolibrary Group Ltd; 112 Photolibrary Group Ltd;
117 Kevin Schafer/Corbis; 125 Roger Tidman/FLPA; 129 jbaram/Fotolia; 131 Martin Harvey/Gallo Images/Corbis; 142 Photolibrary Group Ltd;
163 TopFoto.co.uk; 172 Jurgen & Christine Sohns/FLPA; 174 Mark Newman/FLPA; 178 Jurgen & Christine Sohns/FLPA; 180 Jurgen & Christine
Sohns/FLPA; 183 Photolibrary Group Ltd; 184 Pete Oford/naturepl.com; 185 Pete Oxford/Minden Pictures/FLPA; 189 M. Watson/ardea.com;
191 Gerard Lacz/FLPA; 194 Pete Oxford/Minden Pictures/FLPA; 195(t) Cyril Ruoso/JH Editorial/Minden Pictures/FLPA, (b) Simon Hosking/FLPA;
196 EcoView/Fotolia; 201 Photolibrary Group Ltd; 202 Cyril Ruoso/JH Editorial/Minden Pictures/FLPA; 204 Photolibrary Group Ltd;
208 Photolibrary Group Ltd; 210 Getty Images; 216 Renee Lynn/CORBIS; 218 Michio Hoshino/Minden Pictures/FLPA;
219 Derek Middleton/FLPA; 223 Frank Leonhardt/dpa/Corbis; 224 L Lee Rue/FLPA; 228 Jim Brandenburg/Minden Pictures/FLPA;
230 Photolibrary Group Ltd; 233 Flip Nicklin/Minden Pictures/FLPA; 234 Mike Lane/FLPA; 236(t) Sumio Harada/Minden Pictures/FLPA,
(b) Frans Lanting/FLPA; 237 Photolibrary Group Ltd; 238 Claro Cortes IV/Reuters/Corbis; 239 Terry Whittaker/FLPA;
241 Michael Gore/FLPA; 243 Kevin Schafer/Corbis; 244 Kennan Ward/Corbis; 246 Photolibrary Group Ltd;
251 New Line/Everett/Rex Features; 252 Yva Momatiuk/John Eastcott/Minden Pictures/FLPA; 253 Steve Klaver/Star Ledger/Corbis;
267 Frans Lanting/Minden Pictures/FLPA; 277 Gerard Lacz/FLPA; 290 Rob Reijnen/Foto Natura/FLPA; 291 William Dow/Corbis;
295 Frans Lanting/Minden Pictures/FLPA; 306 Norma Cornes/Fotolia; 310(t) Karl Ammaman/naturepl.com, (b) Steve Meyfroidt/Fotolia;
314 Joël Dallio/Fotolia; 318 Konrad Wothe/Minden Pictures/FLPA; 320 Taolmor/Fotolia; 321 John Downer Productions/naturepl.com;
322 Bhupinder Singh/Fotolia; 324 Dr Dereck Bromhall/OSF; 331 Joël Dallio/Fotolia; 332 Steve Turner/OSF; 334 Jason Maehl/Fotolia;
335(t) Mike Powles/OSF, (b) Reuters/Antony Njuguna; 343 Carlton Mceachern/Fotolia; 351 Bruce Davidson/naturepl.com;
353 Eric Gevaert/Fotolia; 361 Ami Beyer/Fotolia; 363 NHPA/Daniel Heuclin; 365 Mark Moffett/Minden Pictures/FLPA;
366 Reiner Weidemann/Fotolia; 370 FLPA; 377 NHPA/Martin Harvey

All other photographs are from:

Castrol, Corel, digitalSTOCK, digitalvision, John Foxx, Miles Kelly Archives, PhotoAlto,
PhotoDisc, PhotoEssentials, PhotoPro, Stockbyte

Made with paper from a sustainable forest

www.mileskelly.net
info@mileskelly.net

www.factsforprojects.com
The one-stop homework helper – pictures, facts, videos, projects and more

Contents

PENGUINS

HORSES

MONKEYS AND APES

BEARS

BIG CATS

ELEPHANTS

DEADLY CREATURES

Sharks

Delve into the world of sharks and learn all about
these fascinating fish of the deep.

Anatomy • Hunting • The first sharks • Swimming
Weird sharks • Senses • Hammerhead sharks • Babies
Camouflage • Shark attacks • Great white shark
Megamouth shark • Shark relatives

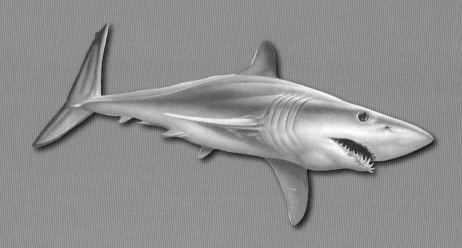

Sharks swarm the seas

Sharks are meat-eating fish, and nearly all of them live in the sea. Every kind of shark is a meat-eater or carnivore. Many are active hunters and chase after their prey. Some lie in wait to grab victims. Others are scavengers, feasting on the dying and dead bodies of animals, such as whales and seals.

▼ The sand tiger has all the typical shark features — beady eyes, nostrils for sensing scents, a wide mouth with sharp teeth, gill slits for underwater breathing, a powerful tail for swimming, fins for steering — and a huge appetite for many kinds of prey!

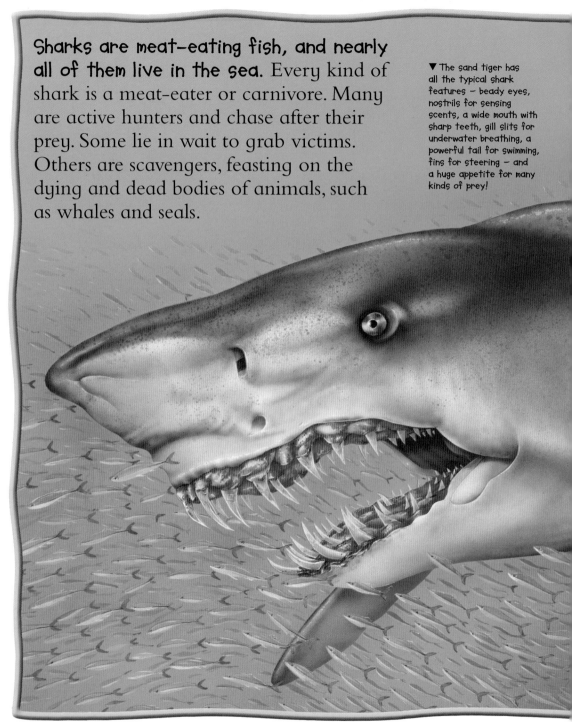

Some sharks are giants

The biggest fish in the world is a type of shark called the whale shark. It grows to 12 metres long, about the same as three family cars end-to-end. It can weigh over 12 tonnes, which is three times heavier than three family cars put together!

Despite the whale shark's huge size, it mostly eats tiny prey. It opens its enormous mouth, takes in a great gulp of water and squeezes it out through the gill slits on either side of its neck. Inside the gills, small animals such as shrimp-like krill, little fish and baby squid are trapped and swallowed.

▶ Krill look like small shrimps and are usually 2 to 3 centimetres long. Millions of them, along with other small creatures, make up plankton.

Whale sharks like cruising across the warm oceans, swimming up to 5000 kilometres in one year. They wander far and wide, but tend to visit the same areas at certain times of year, when their food is plentiful.

▲ The whale shark swims with its mouth wide open to filter krill from the water. It sometimes swallows larger animals, such as penguins, smaller sharks and tuna fish.

Whale sharks may sleep for months! It's thought that they sink to the seabed and lie there, hardly moving, for several weeks each year. This could help them to save energy when food is scarce.

Basking sharks are huge, too. They are the second-biggest of all fish, reaching 10 metres in length and 6 tonnes in weight. Like whale sharks, basking sharks filter small animals and bits of food from the sea.

▲ Ripple patterns on basking sharks are caused by sunlight shining through the waves onto the shark.

Some sharks like to eat stinking, rotting flesh! The Greenland shark eats the meat from all kinds of dead bodies. These include whales, seals, dolphins, other sharks, squid and even drowned animals, such as reindeer.

▶ The Arctic water is very cold, so Greenland sharks can only swim slowly.

Sharks outlived the dinosaurs

The first sharks lived more than 350 million years ago. This was 120 million years before the dinosaurs appeared on Earth. Dinosaurs died out 65 million years ago but sharks survived. So sharks have ruled the seas for over twice as long as dinosaurs ruled the land!

Some prehistoric fish are called 'spiny sharks'. They looked like sharks with streamlined bodies and sharp spikes on their fins and bellies. Their real name is acanthodians, and they lived in lakes and rivers 400 to 250 million years ago.

MAKE MEGALODON'S MOUTH!

You will need:
black pen big cardboard box
large pieces of white card
scissors tape
1. Use a pen to draw a shark's mouth onto the box and cut it out.
2. Draw and cut out 20 teeth shapes.
3. Tape these inside the mouth. Draw on eyes. Now you can stare *Megalodon* in the face!

◀ Sharks' basic body shapes and behaviour have hardly changed since they first appeared. The shark *Hybodus* lived about 160 million years ago in the Jurassic period, during the age of dinosaurs.

Bits of shark have turned to stone!

Parts of sharks that died long ago have been preserved in rocks, as fossils. Most fossils are made of the hard parts, such as teeth and scales. These show the size of the shark and the kind of food it ate.

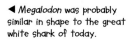

◀ *Megalodon* was probably similar in shape to the great white shark of today.

The biggest shark in history was probably *Megalodon*. Its fossil teeth look like those of the great white shark, but they're twice as big. *Megalodon* could have been 15 or even 20 metres long – three times the size of today's great white. It lived about 20 to 2 million years ago and was one of the greatest hunters the animal world has ever known.

Super swimmers

Nearly all sharks are slim and streamlined, making them fast swimmers. A streamlined shape slips through the water easily and lets the shark travel at speed. One of the fastest sharks is the short-fin mako. It swims at more than 55 kilometres an hour – much faster than a champion human sprinter!

▼ The mako shark is slim and speedy, and races after prey, such as mackerel, tuna and squid. It can leap more than 10 metres out of the water.

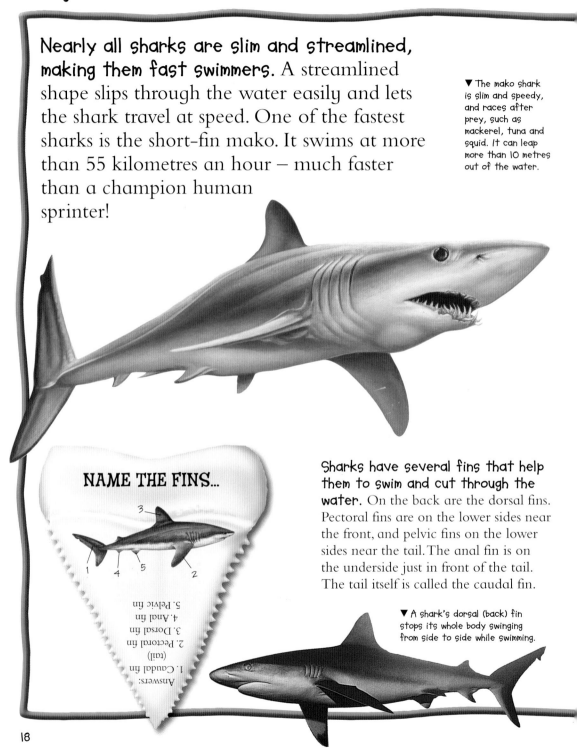

NAME THE FINS...

3
1   4   5   2

Answers:
1. Caudal fin (tail)
2. Pectoral fin
3. Dorsal fin
4. Anal fin
5. Pelvic fin

Sharks have several fins that help them to swim and cut through the water. On the back are the dorsal fins. Pectoral fins are on the lower sides near the front, and pelvic fins on the lower sides near the tail. The anal fin is on the underside just in front of the tail. The tail itself is called the caudal fin.

▼ A shark's dorsal (back) fin stops its whole body swinging from side to side while swimming.

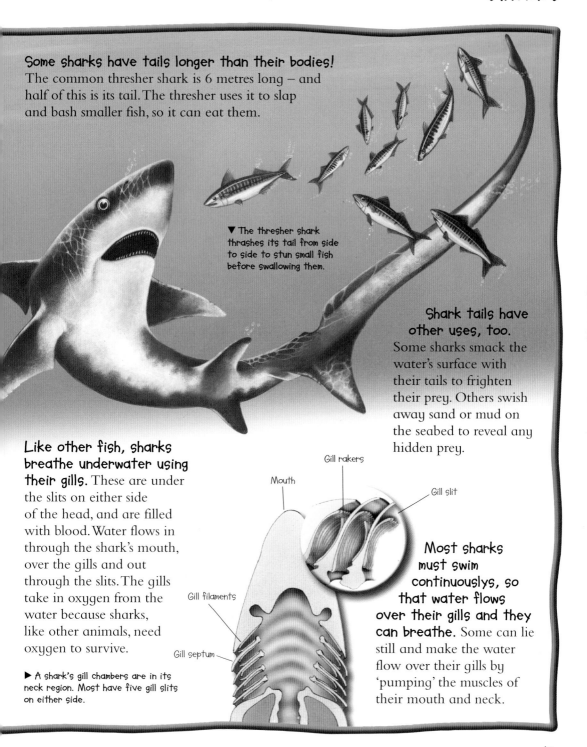

Some sharks have tails longer than their bodies!
The common thresher shark is 6 metres long – and half of this is its tail. The thresher uses it to slap and bash smaller fish, so it can eat them.

▼ The thresher shark thrashes its tail from side to side to stun small fish before swallowing them.

Shark tails have other uses, too. Some sharks smack the water's surface with their tails to frighten their prey. Others swish away sand or mud on the seabed to reveal any hidden prey.

Like other fish, sharks breathe underwater using their gills. These are under the slits on either side of the head, and are filled with blood. Water flows in through the shark's mouth, over the gills and out through the slits. The gills take in oxygen from the water because sharks, like other animals, need oxygen to survive.

▶ A shark's gill chambers are in its neck region. Most have five gill slits on either side.

Gill rakers

Mouth

Gill slit

Gill filaments

Gill septum

Most sharks must swim continuouslys, so that water flows over their gills and they can breathe. Some can lie still and make the water flow over their gills by 'pumping' the muscles of their mouth and neck.

Sharks eat almost anything!

Tiger sharks swallow all kinds of rubbish. This shark is famous for trying to eat nearly everything, in the hope that it might be tasty. However, some of the items it swallows are not even food – such as tin cans and beach shoes!

▶ A hungry tiger shark will try to catch fast, agile prey such as sea lions and seals, biting hard, so their prey bleeds and weakens.

Tiger sharks are cannibals. This means that they eat their own kind, which is quite rare in the animal kingdom.

Young tiger sharks have stripes along their sides, like a real tiger. This helps them to hide, or be camouflaged, among shadows of seaweed and rocks. However, the stripes fade with age and hardly show on the grown-ups.

Tiger sharks swim right up to the beach!
Most sharks stay away from the shore in case
they get stranded and die. But tiger sharks
come near to the shore, especially at
night, to explore for food. They don't
seem to mind swimming in water
that's so shallow, it would hardly
cover your knees. This can make
it dangerous to go paddling!

**I DON'T
BELIEVE IT!**
Tiger sharks
have eaten all kinds
of strange things —
bottles, tools, car tyres,
and in one case, a type of
drum called a tom-tom!

**Most sharks prefer just a few
types of food.** One kind of bullhead
shark likes to eat only sea urchins.
However, if it gets very hungry, it will
try other foods.

**Not all sharks have sharp, pointed
teeth.** The Port Jackson shark has wide,
broad teeth, like rounded pebbles. It uses these
to crush the hard body cases of its favourite
food – shellfish.

Sharks have no bones!

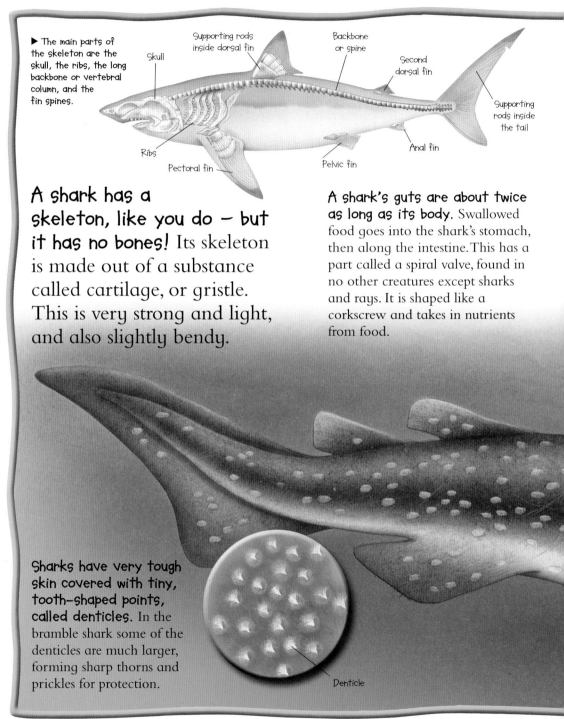

▶ The main parts of the skeleton are the skull, the ribs, the long backbone or vertebral column, and the fin spines.

Skull

Supporting rods inside dorsal fin

Backbone or spine

Second dorsal fin

Supporting rods inside the tail

Ribs

Pectoral fin

Pelvic fin

Anal fin

A shark has a skeleton, like you do – but it has no bones! Its skeleton is made out of a substance called cartilage, or gristle. This is very strong and light, and also slightly bendy.

A shark's guts are about twice as long as its body. Swallowed food goes into the shark's stomach, then along the intestine. This has a part called a spiral valve, found in no other creatures except sharks and rays. It is shaped like a corkscrew and takes in nutrients from food.

Sharks have very tough skin covered with tiny, tooth-shaped points, called denticles. In the bramble shark some of the denticles are much larger, forming sharp thorns and prickles for protection.

Denticle

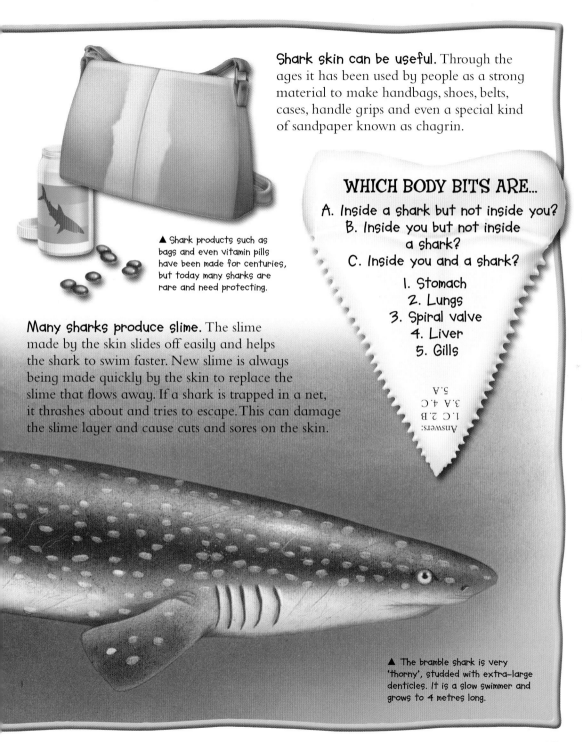

Shark skin can be useful. Through the ages it has been used by people as a strong material to make handbags, shoes, belts, cases, handle grips and even a special kind of sandpaper known as chagrin.

▲ Shark products such as bags and even vitamin pills have been made for centuries, but today many sharks are rare and need protecting.

WHICH BODY BITS ARE...
A. Inside a shark but not inside you?
B. Inside you but not inside a shark?
C. Inside you and a shark?

1. Stomach
2. Lungs
3. Spiral valve
4. Liver
5. Gills

Answers:
1.C 2.B
3.A 4.C
5.A

Many sharks produce slime. The slime made by the skin slides off easily and helps the shark to swim faster. New slime is always being made quickly by the skin to replace the slime that flows away. If a shark is trapped in a net, it thrashes about and tries to escape. This can damage the slime layer and cause cuts and sores on the skin.

▲ The bramble shark is very 'thorny', studded with extra-large denticles. It is a slow swimmer and grows to 4 metres long.

Ultimate killer

The world's biggest predatory, or hunting, fish is the great white shark. In real life it is certainly large – at 6 metres in length and weighing more than one tonne. Great whites live around the world, mainly in warmer seas. They have a fearsome reputation.

▼ Great whites are curious about unfamiliar items in the sea. They often come very close to investigate anti-shark cages and the divers protected inside. This is partly because great whites are always on the lookout for food.

I DON'T BELIEVE IT!

The risk of being struck by lightning is 20 times greater than the risk of being attacked by a shark.

Great whites get hot! This is because they can make their bodies warmer than the surrounding water. This allows their muscles to work more quickly, so they can swim faster and more powerfully. It means the great white is partly 'warm-blooded' like you.

The great white has 50 or more teeth and each one is up to 6 centimetres long. The teeth are razor-sharp but slim, like blades, and they sometimes snap off. But new teeth are always growing just behind, ready to move forward and replace the snapped-off teeth.

The great white 'saws' lumps of food from its victim. Each tooth has tiny sharp points along its edges. As the shark starts to feed, it bites hard and then shakes its head from side to side. The teeth work like rows of small saws to slice off a mouthful.

The great white often attacks unseen from below. It surges up from the dark depths with tremendous power. It can smash into a big prey such as a seal or a dolphin, and lift it right out of the water as it takes its first bite.

Great whites let their victims bleed to death. They bite on their first charge then move off, leaving the victim with terrible wounds. When the injured prey is weak, the great white comes back to devour its meal.

Strange sharks

Six-gill sharks have an extra pair of gills.
This may be the number that ancient sharks
had long ago, before they developed into
modern sharks. Six-gill sharks are up to
5 metres long and eat various foods,
from shellfish to dead dolphins.

▶ Each tooth of the frilled
shark has three needle-like
points for grabbing
soft-bodied prey.

**I DON'T
BELIEVE IT!**

The smallest
sharks could lie
curled up in your
hand. The dwarf
lanternshark is just
20 centimetres long.

Some sharks are frilly. The frilled shark has
six pairs of wavy gill slits. It looks more like an eel
than a shark, with a slim body 2 metres in length, and
long frilly fins. It is dark brown in colour, lives in very
deep waters and eats squid and octopus.

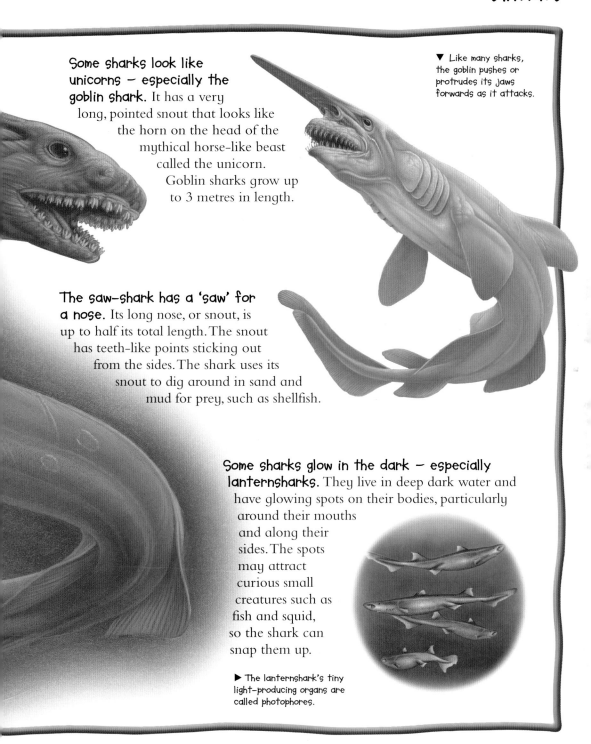

Some sharks look like unicorns — especially the goblin shark. It has a very long, pointed snout that looks like the horn on the head of the mythical horse-like beast called the unicorn. Goblin sharks grow up to 3 metres in length.

▼ Like many sharks, the goblin pushes or protrudes its jaws forwards as it attacks.

The saw-shark has a 'saw' for a nose. Its long nose, or snout, is up to half its total length. The snout has teeth-like points sticking out from the sides. The shark uses its snout to dig around in sand and mud for prey, such as shellfish.

Some sharks glow in the dark — especially lanternsharks. They live in deep dark water and have glowing spots on their bodies, particularly around their mouths and along their sides. The spots may attract curious small creatures such as fish and squid, so the shark can snap them up.

► The lanternshark's tiny light-producing organs are called photophores.

Sharks are sensitive!

Most sharks have big eyes and can see well, especially in the dark. Many feed at night, or in deeper water where there's little light. This makes eyesight especially important to the shark so that it can spot its prey. Some sharks have eyes that glow in the dark, like a cat's.

▼ A porbeagle shark uses its keen eyesight to chase its favourite food — mackerel.

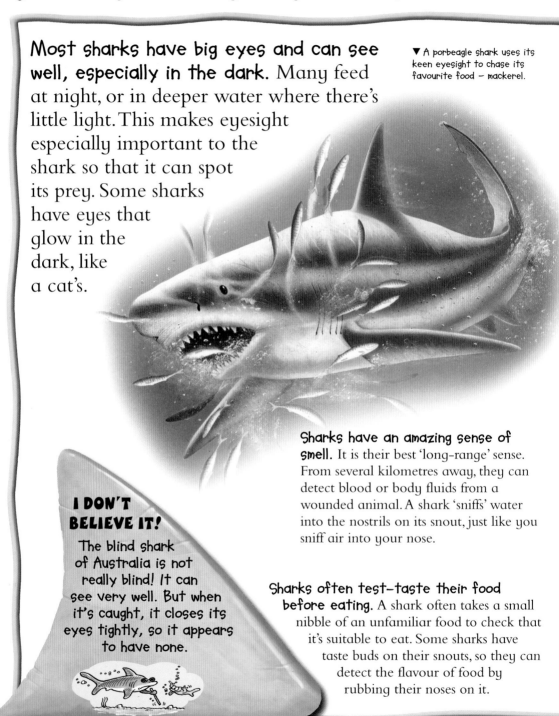

Sharks have an amazing sense of smell. It is their best 'long-range' sense. From several kilometres away, they can detect blood or body fluids from a wounded animal. A shark 'sniffs' water into the nostrils on its snout, just like you sniff air into your nose.

I DON'T BELIEVE IT!

The blind shark of Australia is not really blind! It can see very well. But when it's caught, it closes its eyes tightly, so it appears to have none.

Sharks often test-taste their food before eating. A shark often takes a small nibble of an unfamiliar food to check that it's suitable to eat. Some sharks have taste buds on their snouts, so they can detect the flavour of food by rubbing their noses on it.

Sharks can feel their way through narrow gaps in the dark using the sense of touch on their skin. There is also a narrow strip along each side of a shark's body called the lateral line. It can sense ripples and currents in the water from animals moving nearby.

Lateral line

▲ The lateral line runs along the side of the body from head to tail base.

Sharks can hear divers breathing! They detect the sound of air bubbles coming from scuba-divers' mouths. But hearing is not the shark's best sense. Its ear openings are tiny, usually just behind the eyes.

▼ The electricity-sensing ampullae of Lorenzini show up as tiny holes over this great white's snout.

Sharks can detect electricity. As sea animals move, their muscles give off tiny pulses of electricity into the water. A shark has hundreds of tiny pits over its snout called ampullae of Lorenzini. These 'feel' the electric pulses. A shark can even detect prey buried out of sight in mud.

Hammers for heads

The hammerhead shark really does have a hammer-like head. Experts suggest several reasons for this strange shape. One is that the head is shaped like the wings of a plane. As the shark swims, water flowing over its head helps to keep its front end lifted up, rather than nose-diving – just as wings keep a plane in the air.

▲ The hammerhead's eyes, nostrils and electricity-sensing organs are at each end of the wing-shaped head.

The hammer-shaped head may improve the shark's senses. The nostrils are at each end of the 'hammer'. Smells drifting from the side reach one nostril well before the other. By swinging its head from side to side, the hammerhead can pinpoint the direction of a smell more quickly.

▼ Hammerheads often swim close to the seabed, searching for buried fish and shellfish.

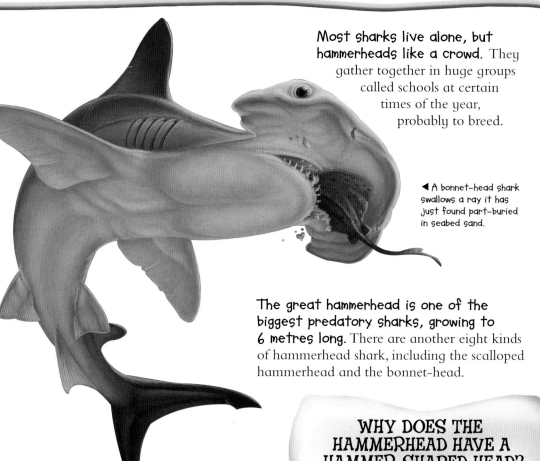

Most sharks live alone, but hammerheads like a crowd. They gather together in huge groups called schools at certain times of the year, probably to breed.

◀ A bonnet-head shark swallows a ray it has just found part-buried in seabed sand.

The great hammerhead is one of the biggest predatory sharks, growing to 6 metres long. There are another eight kinds of hammerhead shark, including the scalloped hammerhead and the bonnet-head.

Hammerheads are among the most dangerous sharks. They have been known to attack people, although their usual food includes fish, squid, crabs and shellfish. They eat stingrays too and don't seem to be affected by the painful sting. However, hammerheads are themselves eaten – by people. They are caught and cut up for their tasty meat and for the thick oil from their livers.

WHY DOES THE HAMMERHEAD HAVE A HAMMER-SHAPED HEAD?

1. To break apart rocks to get at prey behind them.
2. To help sense the direction of smells in the water.
3. To smash open windows in shipwrecks.

Answer:
2

Big mouth

The megamouth shark was discovered in 1976 near Hawaii in the Pacific Ocean. An American research ship hauled in its parachute-like anchor to find a strange shark tangled in it. Experts knew at once that this was a new type of shark, never described before.

Megamouths open their great mouths as they swim through shoals of small sea creatures, such as krill and young fish. The little prey get trapped inside the mouth and swallowed. The megamouth is not really an active hunter. It is a slow-swimming filter-feeder, like the whale shark and the basking shark.

The megamouth, as its name suggests, has a massive mouth more than 1.3 metres wide. Its soft, flabby body is about 5 metres long. In the summer when the megamouth has been feeding well, it can weigh more than one tonne.

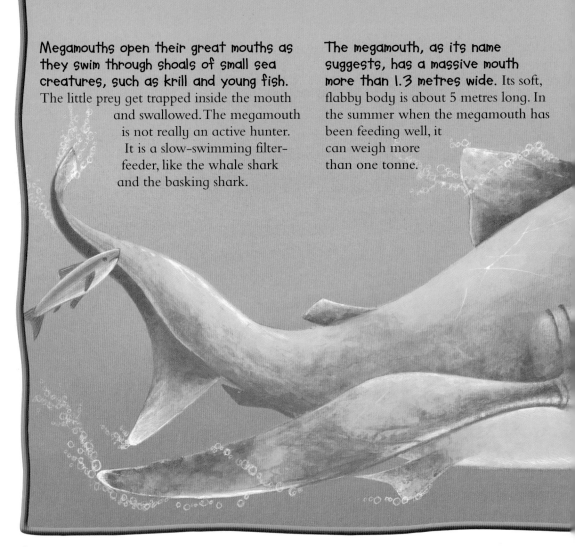

Megamouths go up and down every day. They rise near the surface at dusk in order to feed during the night. At dawn they sink to deeper waters and spend the day in the dark, more than 200 metres down.

Megamouths are scattered around the world. They have been caught in all the tropical oceans, especially in the Western Pacific and Indian oceans. Only 20 or so have been found in the past 30 years. It may be that there have never been many megamouths in the world.

▼ The megamouth's huge jaws are right at the front of its body, not slung under the head as in most sharks.

The megamouth's mouth glows in the dark depths of the sea. Despite the vast size of the mouth, the teeth are tiny.

Scientists believe that there may be more types of shark as yet undiscovered. Sometimes the badly-rotted bodies of strange sharks are washed up onto beaches. But the remains are often too decayed to be identified.

The loose skin and floppy fins show that the megamouth is a slow swimmer.

Swimming with sharks

▼ This great white shark is about to take a bite out of a piece of meat dangled from a boat. Although it's not hunting, you can see how it lifts its snout up high and thrusts its teeth forward to attack.

Some small types of shark are fairly safe and people can swim near them with care. In some tourist areas, people can even feed sharks. The sharks seem to become trained to accept food from divers.

The cookie-cutter shark is only 50 centimetres long, with a large mouth and big, sharp teeth. This shark attacks fish much larger than itself, biting out small patches of skin and flesh, before racing away. Its victim is left with a neat round hole on its body – ouch!

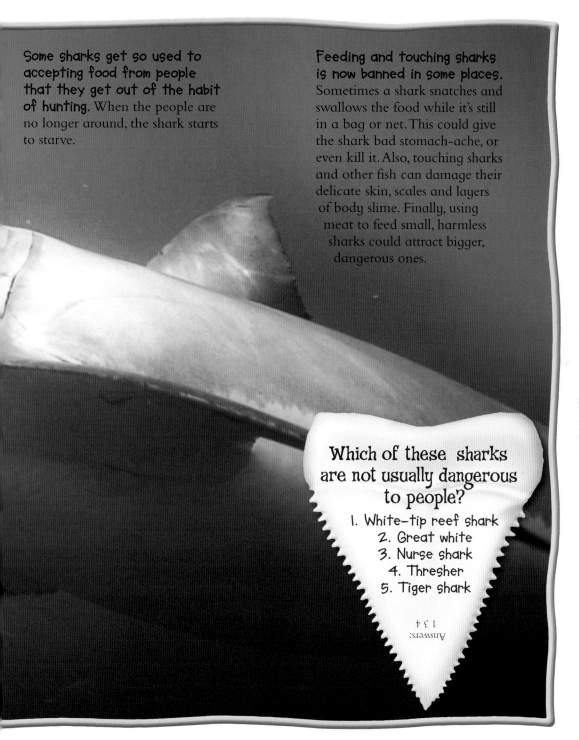

Some sharks get so used to accepting food from people that they get out of the habit of hunting. When the people are no longer around, the shark starts to starve.

Feeding and touching sharks is now banned in some places. Sometimes a shark snatches and swallows the food while it's still in a bag or net. This could give the shark bad stomach-ache, or even kill it. Also, touching sharks and other fish can damage their delicate skin, scales and layers of body slime. Finally, using meat to feed small, harmless sharks could attract bigger, dangerous ones.

Which of these sharks are not usually dangerous to people?

1. White-tip reef shark
2. Great white
3. Nurse shark
4. Thresher
5. Tiger shark

Answers:
1 3 4

Shark cousins

Sharks have many close relations who, like themselves, have a skeleton made of cartilage rather than bone. Other kinds of cartilaginous fish include skates and rays, and the deep-water ratfish, or chimaera.

Skates and rays are flat fish, but not flatfish. True flatfish, such as plaice, have bony skeletons and lie on their left or right side. Skates and rays have very wide bodies with flattened upper and lower surfaces, and a long narrow tail.

▲ Chimaeras are also called ratfish after their long, tapering tails. Most are about one metre long.

A ray or skate 'flies' through the water. The sides of its body extend out like wings. The 'wings' push the water backwards, and so the ray or skate swims forwards. Unlike sharks and other fish, the ray's tail is seldom used for swimming.

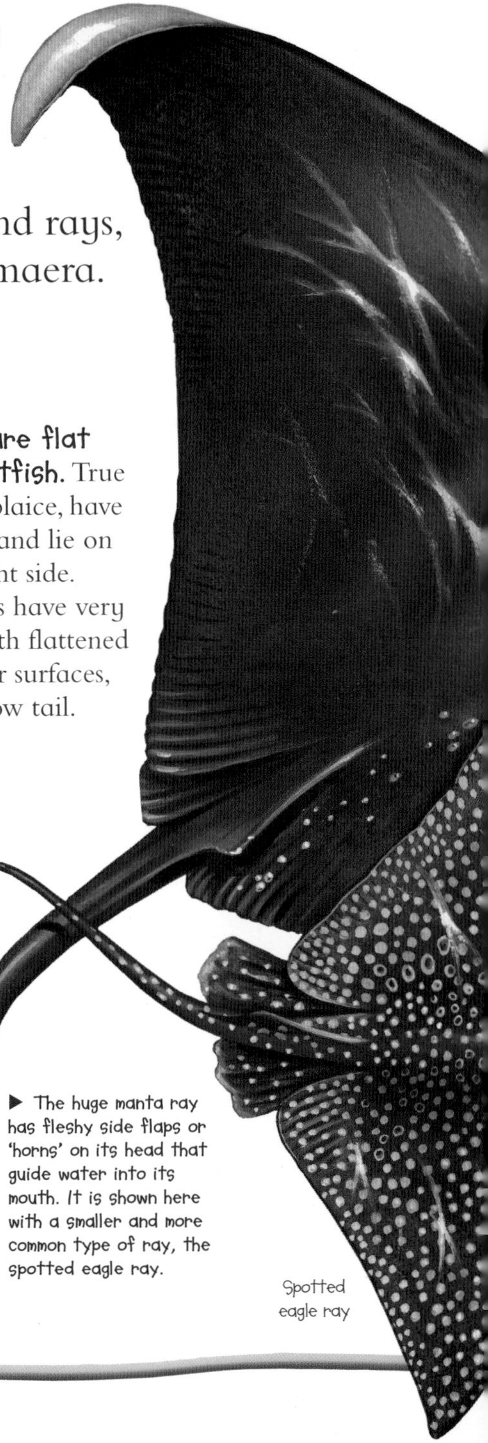

▶ The huge manta ray has fleshy side flaps or 'horns' on its head that guide water into its mouth. It is shown here with a smaller and more common type of ray, the spotted eagle ray.

Spotted eagle ray

The biggest rays are mantas. They measure up to 7 metres across and weigh nearly 2 tonnes. Manta rays have huge mouths and feed like whale sharks by filtering small creatures from the water. Despite their great size, mantas can leap clear of the surface and crash back with a tremendous splash.

Stingrays have sharp spines on their long tails. They use them like daggers to jab poison into enemies or victims. Some stingrays live in lakes and rivers.

Sawfish are different from saw-sharks. A sawfish is shaped like a shark, but is a type of ray with a long snout edged by pointed teeth. You can tell the difference between them because a sawfish has gill slits on the bottom of its body, rather than on the side.

Manta ray

THE 'FLYING' RAY

You will need:
scissors stiff paper coloured pens
sticky tape drinking straw
modelling clay

1. Cut out a ray shape from paper.
2. Colour it brightly. Fold it along the middle so the 'wings' angle upwards. Stick the straw along the underside, so part sticks out as a 'tail'. Add a blob of modelling clay to one end.
3. Launch your 'flying ray' into the air. Adjust the tail weight until it glides smoothly.

Sharks need partners

▼ A blue shark heads towards its traditional breeding area in a shallow part of the ocean near the coast to search for a mate.

Female sharks need male sharks of the same breed to produce young. When a male and a female get together, they mate. Then the female can produce offspring. Some types of shark lay eggs, while others give birth to live young.

Some sharks gather in large groups, or shoals, to breed. Hammerheads come together in hundreds or even thousands, so the females and males can choose partners for mating. Bonnet-heads, nurse and dogfish sharks also form breeding shoals.

▼ Hammerheads swim slowly in huge shoals at breeding time.

▼ Male white-tip reef sharks rest in the shallows, waiting for scents called pheromones to drift through the water, which tell them that females are nearby.

Sharks have a complicated way of getting together, known as courtship. They give off scents or 'perfumes' into the water to attract a partner. Then the two rub one another, wind their bodies around each other, and maybe even bite the other! The male may hold the female using his claspers, which are two long parts on his underside.

Some sharks don't breed very often. This can cause problems, especially when people catch too many of them. The sharks cannot breed fast enough to keep up their numbers, and they become rare and endangered.

Eggs and baby sharks

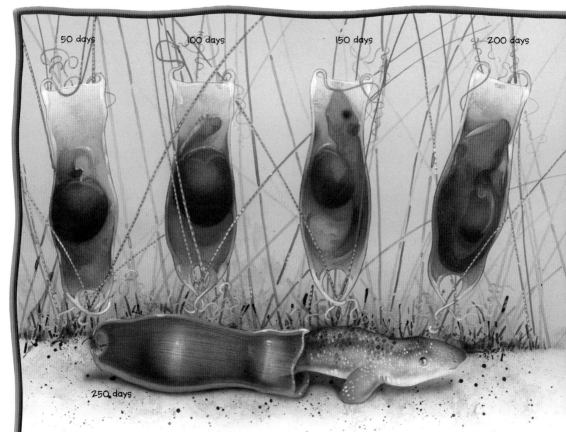

50 days

100 days

150 days

200 days

250 days

▲ A baby catshark develops slowly in its protective case. At 50 days it is smaller than its store of food, the yolk. It gradually develops and finally hatches eight months later.

Some mother sharks lay eggs. Each egg has a strong case with a developing baby shark, called an embryo, inside. The case has long threads, which stick to seaweed or rocks. Look out for empty egg cases on beaches. They are known as 'mermaids' purses'.

Some mother sharks do not lay eggs, but give birth to baby sharks, which are known as pups. The hammerhead and the basking shark do this. The pups have to look after themselves straight away. Shark parents do not care for their young.

Some sharks have hundreds of babies at once! The whale shark may give birth to as many as 300 pups, each about 60 centimetres long.

▲ A lanternshark baby, or pup, still attached to its yolk, which continues to nourish its growth.

Sadly, most young sharks die. The mothers lay eggs or give birth in sheltered places such as bays, inlets and reefs, where there are plenty of places to hide. But the young sharks are easy prey for hunters, such as dolphins, barracudas, sea lions – and other sharks.

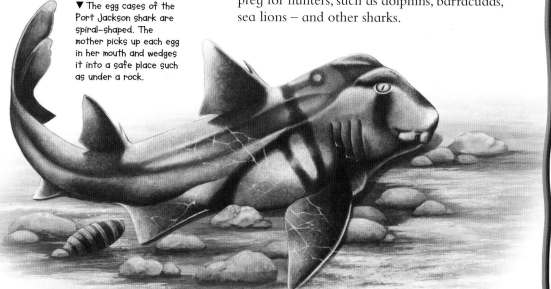

▼ The egg cases of the Port Jackson shark are spiral-shaped. The mother picks up each egg in her mouth and wedges it into a safe place such as under a rock.

Sharks can 'disappear'

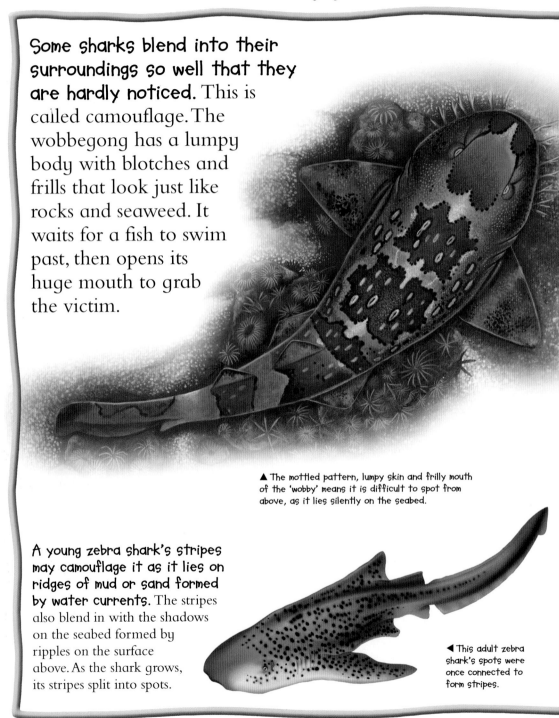

Some sharks blend into their surroundings so well that they are hardly noticed. This is called camouflage. The wobbegong has a lumpy body with blotches and frills that look just like rocks and seaweed. It waits for a fish to swim past, then opens its huge mouth to grab the victim.

▲ The mottled pattern, lumpy skin and frilly mouth of the 'wobby' means it is difficult to spot from above, as it lies silently on the seabed.

A young zebra shark's stripes may camouflage it as it lies on ridges of mud or sand formed by water currents. The stripes also blend in with the shadows on the seabed formed by ripples on the surface above. As the shark grows, its stripes split into spots.

◄ This adult zebra shark's spots were once connected to form stripes.

Angel sharks have wide, flat bodies the same colour as sand. They blend perfectly into the sandy seabed as they lie in wait for prey. They are called 'angel' sharks because their fins spread wide like an angel's wings.

▶ The flattened body of the angel shark looks like a low lump in the sandy seabed.

Even in the open ocean, sharks can be hard to spot. This is because of the way they are coloured, known as countershading. The shark's back is darker while its underside is lighter. Seen from above the dark back blends in with the gloom of deeper water below. Seen from below the pale belly merges with the brighter water's surface and sky above.

▼ A side view of this silvertip shark shows countershading — darker back, lighter underside.

WHICH SHARKS LIVE WHERE?

Pair up these sharks and the habitats in which live.
1. Blue shark — light blue above, mainly white below
2. Wobbegong — green and brown blotches, lumps and frills
3. Spotted dogfish — dark blotches on light body
Habitats:
A. Sandy seabed
B. Open ocean
C. Rocks and weeds

Answers:
1 B
2 C 3 A

43

Sharks on the move

There are about 330 kinds of sharks, but only a few leave the salty water of the sea and swim into the fresh water of rivers. One is the bull shark, which travels hundreds of kilometres up rivers, especially in South America. It has attacked people fishing, washing or boating in lakes.

The most common sharks are blue sharks, which are found in almost every part of every ocean except the icy polar seas. In the Atlantic Ocean, they travel from the Caribbean to Western Europe, down to Africa, and back to the Caribbean – 6000 kilometres in one year!

Some sharks live in small areas and rarely stray outside them. One is the Galapagos shark, which swims around a few small groups of mid-ocean islands in the tropics.

▼ Not all sharks travel far afield. The Galapagos shark stays close to home, swimming only in one small area.

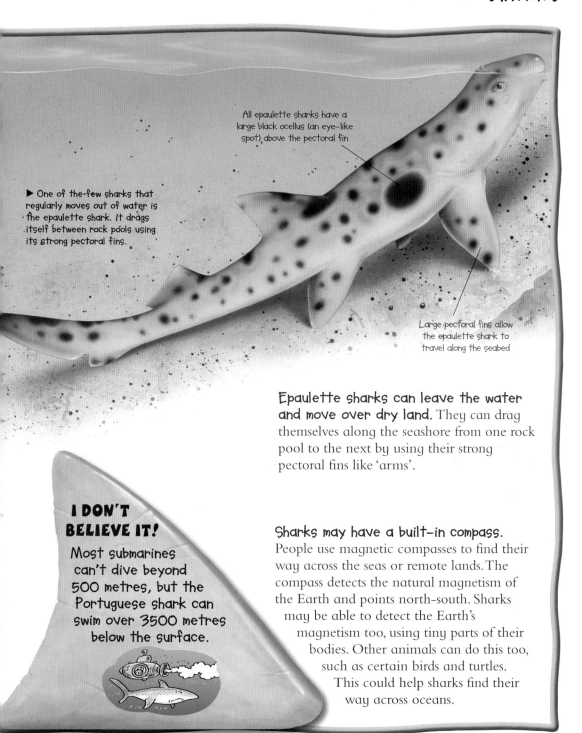

All epaulette sharks have a large black ocellus (an eye-like spot) above the pectoral fin

► One of the few sharks that regularly moves out of water is the epaulette shark. It drags itself between rock pools using its strong pectoral fins.

Large pectoral fins allow the epaulette shark to travel along the seabed

Epaulette sharks can leave the water and move over dry land. They can drag themselves along the seashore from one rock pool to the next by using their strong pectoral fins like 'arms'.

I DON'T BELIEVE IT!

Most submarines can't dive beyond 500 metres, but the Portuguese shark can swim over 3500 metres below the surface.

Sharks may have a built-in compass. People use magnetic compasses to find their way across the seas or remote lands. The compass detects the natural magnetism of the Earth and points north-south. Sharks may be able to detect the Earth's magnetism too, using tiny parts of their bodies. Other animals can do this too, such as certain birds and turtles. This could help sharks find their way across oceans.

Science and sharks

Scientists study sharks around the world — especially how they live, behave and travel. Small radio-transmitter trackers can be attached to big sharks and the radio signals show where the shark roams. Smaller sharks have littl plastic tags with letters and numbers attached to their fins. If the shark is caught again, its code can be traced.

▲ This dogfish shark has a plastic tag fixed to its dorsal fin, so scientists can record its travels.

Sharks show us problems in the oceans. In some areas, sharks have disappeared for no obvious reason. This might suggest chemicals and pollution in the water, which upset the balance of nature. The chemicals could affect the sharks themselves, making them feel unwell so that they travel away. Or the pollution could affect the sharks' prey, such as small fish. Then the sharks have to hunt elsewhere for food.

▼ Huge aquariums let us watch the fascinating underwater world of sharks and other fish.

Some sharks can live in captivity. They are very popular with visitors to sea-life centres and aquariums. People love to get up close to sharks and see their teeth, eyes, fins, and their grace and power as they swim. The captured animals can also help us to learn more about the species and how to protect them and their natural habitats.

Sharks may help us to find new medicines. Sharks seem to suffer from diseases and infections quite rarely compared to other animals. Scientists are examining their body parts, blood and the natural chemicals they produce in order to make better medical drugs for humans.

Shark attacks

▲ From below, a surfboard looks similar to a seal or a turtle, which may be the reason why large hunting sharks sometimes attack surfers.

The most dangerous sharks include the great white, tiger and bull sharks. However, a shark that attacks a person might not be properly identified. Attacks happen very quickly and the shark is soon gone. Some attacks blamed on great whites might well have been made by bull sharks instead.

▼ Great whites do sometimes attack humans, but their favourite foods are fish, seals and sealions.

Areas of the world known for shark attacks include the east coast of North America, the west coast of Africa and around Southeast Asia and Australia. This is partly because these places are popular with swimmers and surfers.

Most shark attacks are not fatal. A shark may 'test-bite' a person and realize that this is not its usual prey. The victim may be injured, but not killed.

◀ Even quite large sharks are themselves hunted, by the huge elephant seal, which can weigh up to 5 tonnes.

Sharks do not attack people because they hate us. They are simply hungry and looking for a meal. They may sometimes mistake humans for their usual prey, such as sea lions.

The dangers of shark attacks can be reduced in many ways. Examples include shark barriers or nets around the beach, patrols by boats and planes, lookout towers, and only swimming in protected areas between flags.

▶ Movies about sharks often make them seem more eager to attack than in reality. The 1999 film *Deep Blue Sea* features blood-thirsty ultra-intelligent sharks.

I DON'T BELIEVE IT!

Each year there are less than ten fatal shark attacks — ten times less than the number of people killed by falling coconuts!

Sharks are not the most dangerous animals, by a long way! Each year, many more people are killed by poisonous snakes, tigers, elephants, hippos and crocodiles. Some tiny animals are much more lethal. Mosquitoes spread the disease malaria, which kills more than one million people every year.

Save our sharks

Some sharks have become very rare. They include the most feared of all, the great white. There are many reasons – hunting by people who think that all sharks are dangerous, sports angling where people use rods and lines to hook sharks, pollution, catching sharks for people to eat, and catching sharks by accident in nets meant for other fish such as tuna.

Sharks are made into many foods, including shark's-fin soup. Many other shark parts are eaten by people around the world, including the flesh as shark steaks, and the liver and other body parts in various oils, cosmetics and health foods. Sometimes, it's not obvious because names are changed. Meat from the small dogfish shark may be sold as 'rock salmon' or 'rock cod'.

▲ By getting very close to sharks, and studying their detailed behaviour, experts can help the conservation effort.

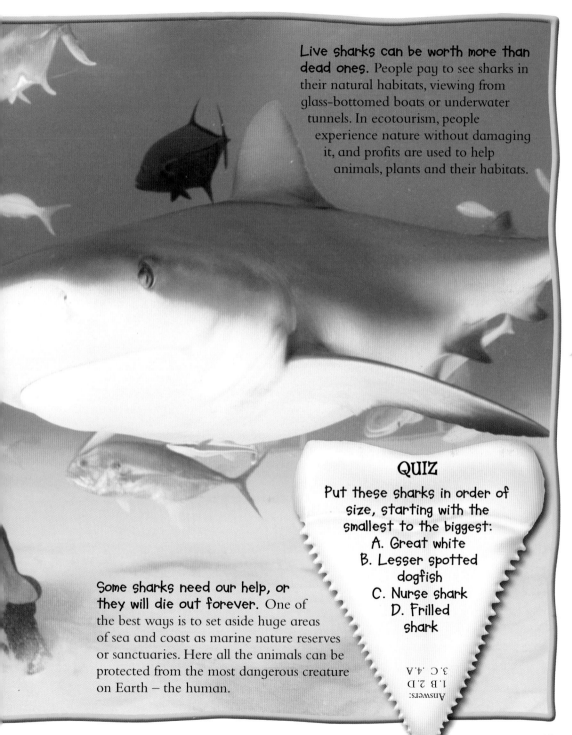

Live sharks can be worth more than dead ones. People pay to see sharks in their natural habitats, viewing from glass-bottomed boats or underwater tunnels. In ecotourism, people experience nature without damaging it, and profits are used to help animals, plants and their habitats.

Some sharks need our help, or they will die out forever. One of the best ways is to set aside huge areas of sea and coast as marine nature reserves or sanctuaries. Here all the animals can be protected from the most dangerous creature on Earth – the human.

QUIZ

Put these sharks in order of size, starting with the smallest to the biggest:
A. Great white
B. Lesser spotted dogfish
C. Nurse shark
D. Frilled shark

Answers:
1.B 2.D
3.C 4.A

51

Whales and Dolphins

Discover the amazing lives of whales and dolphins
and learn all about their beautiful habitats.

Porpoises • Skeletons • Flippers and fins • Senses
Migration • Blue whale • Killer whale • River dolphin
Breathing • Diving • Hunting • Echolocation
Singing • Feeding • Babies

Whales and dolphins are warm!

Welcome to the watery world of whales, dolphins and porpoises. Just like humans, these unusual creatures breathe air and are warm blooded. This is because they belong to the mammal group. All whales, dolphins and porpoises eat animal prey of some kind, rather than plant food. Almost all live in the sea, with just a few kinds of dolphin living in freshwater rivers and lakes. This amazing group of marine mammals also holds many records – the biggest animal in the world, the largest hunter, and some of the fastest, deepest-diving and cleverest creatures ever to have lived.

▶ Many kinds of dolphin live in groups called schools. Common dolphins are colourful, with yellow or tan patches along their sides and dark 'spectacles' around their eyes.

The greatest animals

Whales are the biggest kind of animal in the world today. Some are longer and heavier than the largest trucks. They need a lot of muscle power and energy to move such large bodies. As they live in the ocean, the water helps to support their enormous bulk.

The blue whale is the largest animal ever to have lived. It can grow up to 30 metres in length, which is as long as seven cars placed end to end. It reaches up to 150 tonnes in weight – that's as heavy as 2000 adults or 35 elephants.

On land, bears and tigers are the biggest hunting animals. However, the sperm whale is more than 100 times larger, and easily the biggest predator (active hunter) on Earth. It grows up to 20 metres in length and 50 tonnes in weight.

The animal with the largest mouth is also a whale, called the bowhead. Its whole body is 18 metres in length, and its mouth makes up almost one-third of this. If the bowhead whale opened its mouth wide, it could fit 20 people inside.

Whales breathe air like humans. They must hold their breath as they dive underwater to feed. A few of them, such as the bottlenose whale, can stay underwater for more than one hour. Most humans have trouble holding their breath for even one minute!

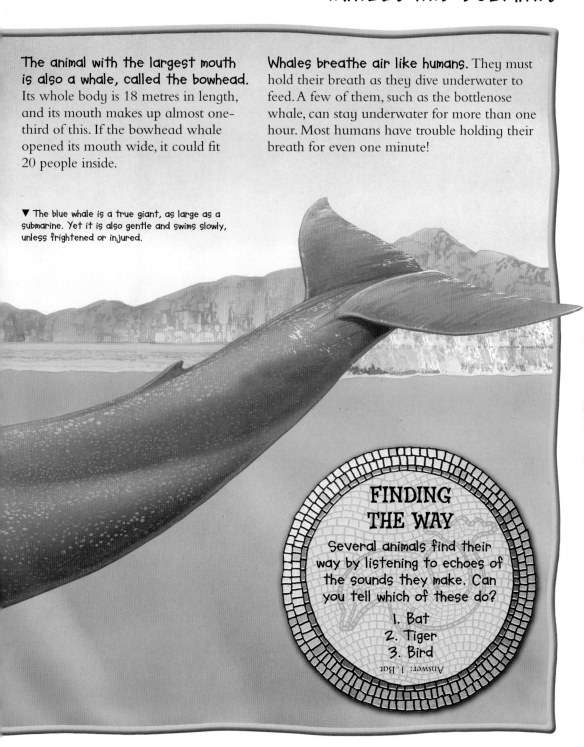

▼ The blue whale is a true giant, as large as a submarine. Yet it is also gentle and swims slowly, unless frightened or injured.

FINDING THE WAY

Several animals find their way by listening to echoes of the sounds they make. Can you tell which of these do?

1. Bat
2. Tiger
3. Bird

Answer: 1. Bat

One big family

The mammal group of cetaceans is made up of about 80 kinds of whale, dolphin and porpoise. The whale group is divided into two main types – baleen whales and toothed whales.

Baleen whales are the largest members of the cetacean group and are often called great whales. They catch food with long strips in their mouths called baleen or whalebone. One example is the sei whale, which is about 16 metres in length and can reach a weight of 25 tonnes.

▲ The sperm whale is the biggest toothed whale. It only seems to have teeth in its lower jaw because those in its upper jaw can barely be seen.

CREATE A DOLPHIN!

You will need:
paper   coloured pens or pencils

Draw a dolphin outline and colour it any pattern you wish. You can name it after its colour, such as the pink-spotted dolphin. Or use your own name, like Amanda's dolphin.

Toothed whales catch prey with their sharp teeth. This subgroup includes sperm whales, beaked whales and pilot whales. One example is the beluga, also known as the white whale. It lives in the cold waters of the Arctic and can grow up to 5 metres in length. It is one of the noisiest whales, making clicks, squeaks and trills.

▼ The finless porpoise, with its blunt 'beak' and bulging forehead, is one of the smallest cetaceans at about 1.5 metres in length.

Another group is made up of beaked whales. These are medium-sized whales with long, beak-shaped mouths. There are about 20 kinds, but some are very rare and hardly ever seen. The shepherd's beaked whale, which is about 7 metres in length, has been seen fewer than 20 times.

There are six species of porpoise. They are usually quite small, at 2 metres or less in length. They have blunter, more rounded heads than dolphins. The finless porpoise, as its name suggests, has a smooth back with no fin.

▼ The dusky dolphin is very inquisitive and likes to swim and leap near boats, perhaps in the hope of being fed.

There are more than 35 kinds of dolphin. Most of them are 2 to 3 metres in length. They are fast swimmers and can often be seen leaping above the waves. The dusky dolphin is one of the highest leapers, twisting and somersaulting before it splashes back into the sea.

Inside whales and dolphins

Whales, dolphins and porpoises are mammals, like humans. They have the same parts inside their bodies as humans. These include bones to make up the skeleton, lots of muscles, a stomach to hold food, a heart to pump blood, and lungs to breathe air.

Most mammals have hair or fur, including humans. Whales, dolphins and porpoises are unusual because they have smooth, hairless skin to help them slip easily through the water. Only a few hairs, mainly bristles, can be found around the eyes, nose and mouth.

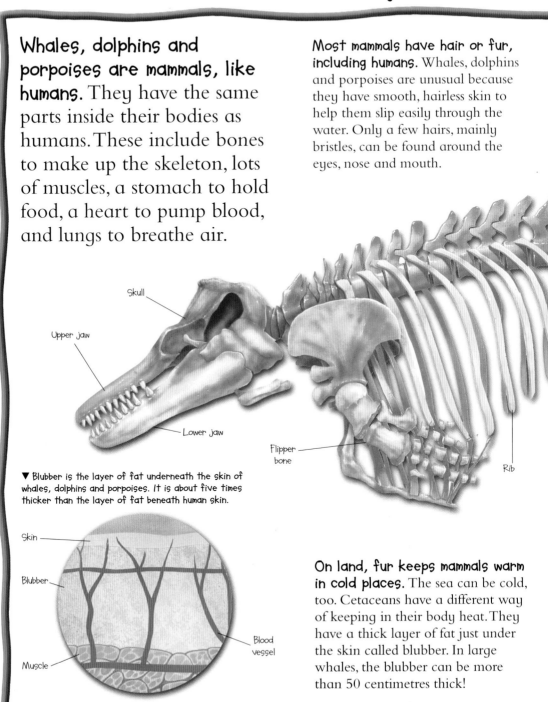

Skull

Upper jaw

Lower jaw

Flipper bone

Rib

▼ Blubber is the layer of fat underneath the skin of whales, dolphins and porpoises. It is about five times thicker than the layer of fat beneath human skin.

Skin

Blubber

Muscle

Blood vessel

On land, fur keeps mammals warm in cold places. The sea can be cold, too. Cetaceans have a different way of keeping in their body heat. They have a thick layer of fat just under the skin called blubber. In large whales, the blubber can be more than 50 centimetres thick!

Cetaceans often have small animals growing inside their bodies called parasites, such as lice. Parasites aren't needed for survival – the whale or dolphin provides them with food. Some baleen whales have their heads covered with barnacles (shellfish), which normally grow on seaside rocks.

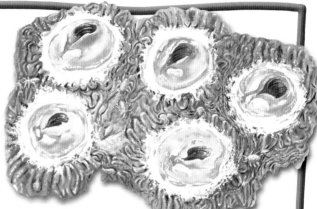

▲ Barnacles are a type of shellfish. They stick firmly to large whales and cannot be rubbed off!

Backbone (vertebra)

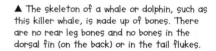

▲ The skeleton of a whale or dolphin, such as this killer whale, is made up of bones. There are no rear leg bones and no bones in the dorsal fin (on the back) or in the tail flukes.

I DON'T BELIEVE IT!

The sperm whale has the biggest brain in the world. It weighs about 8 kilograms – that's over five times the size of a human brain. As far as scientists know, the sperm whale is not the cleverest animal.

Compared to most animals, whales, dolphins and porpoises have large brains for their size. Dolphins are clever creatures, able to learn tricks and solve simple puzzles. Some scientists believe that dolphins have even developed their own language.

Flippers, flukes and fins

Most mammals have four legs and a tail. Whales, dolphins and porpoises don't. They have flippers, a fin and a tail. Flippers are their front limbs, similar to human arms. In fact, flipper bones and human arm and hand bones are alike. Flippers are mainly used for swimming, scratching and waving to send messages to others in the group.

The tail of a cetacean is in two almost identical parts. Each part is called a fluke. Unlike the flippers, flukes have no bones. They are used for swimming as the body arches powerfully to swish them up and down. They can also be slapped onto the water's surface to send messages to other whales. This is called lobtailing.

▼ Whales can often be seen splashing backwards into the water. This is known as breaching. Even the massive humpback whale can breach – and it weighs more than 30 tonnes!

▼ The humpback whale waves its flippers in the air and splashes them onto the surface. This is called flipper-slapping.

The fin on the back of many whales, dolphins and porpoises is known as a dorsal fin. In some, such as the killer whale, it is tall and narrow. In others, such as the bottlenose dolphin, it is shaped like a swept-back triangle. The blue whale has a tiny dorsal fin near its tail. Right whales, the bowhead, beluga and narwhal have no dorsal fin at all.

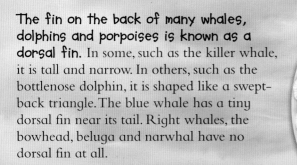

MAKE A WHALE!

You will need:

long balloon   newspaper strips
paints   papier-mâché paste

Paste three layers of newspaper onto the balloon. Let it dry, then paint the whale and stick on paper fins and a tail.

Many whales, dolphins and porpoises jump out of the water and crash back down with a big splash. This is called breaching. It may be done to send a loud message to others in the group, or to try and get rid of skin pests, such as barnacles and whale lice.

Sensitive senses

Whales, dolphins and porpoises have most of the same senses as humans, such as sight and hearing. These senses detect very different surroundings when used in the water, compared to on land. For example, a whale's eyes are similar to a human's, but they have adapted to cope with underwater conditions. Although the water may be murky, cetaceans can see much further in water than humans.

◀ The killer whale spyhops – looks across the surface of the water – for the fins of others in their group or for signs of enemies, such as sharks.

There's one sense that humans don't have, but whales, dolphins and porpoises do – the ability to detect magnetism. Some whales may 'feel' the Earth's weak magnetic force, which humans would detect using a compass. This magnetic sense may help them to find their way on their long journeys, or migrations, through the wide and featureless ocean.

◄ Atlantic spotted dolphins roll over and rub each other. It's like saying, "Hello, we're in the same school."

Whales, dolphins and porpoises have very sensitive skin, so the sense of touch is important to them. They rub and stroke others in their group, or a partner during breeding time. A mother whale often caresses her baby to provide comfort and warmth.

Cetaceans have a weak sense of smell, if any at all. Dolphins use their strong sense of taste to tell them about the foods they are eating. It also means that they can taste the water, too. This lets them know what other bits of food might be drifting nearby!

Hearing is vital for whales, dolphins and porpoises. They don't have ear flaps or outer ears, like humans. Instead, sounds in the water are detected inside the head in the same way that the human inner ear works. Many toothed whales find their way in dark water by making clicking sounds, then listening to the echoes that bounce off nearby objects, such as rocks. This method is called echolocation.

Breathing and diving

Whales, dolphins and porpoises breathe air in and out of their lungs. They don't have gills to breathe underwater, like a fish, so they must hold their breath when diving. Air goes in and out of their body through the blowholes – small openings on top of the head, just in front of the eyes. They work like human nostrils, just in a different place on the head!

▲ As a whale breathes out, its 'blow' often looks like a steamy fountain of water. It can be seen far away across the ocean – and on a calm day, it can be heard from a distance, too.

When a whale comes to the surface after a dive, it breathes out air hard and fast. The moist air, mixed with slimy mucus from the whale's breathing passages, turns into water droplets. This makes the whale's breath look like a jet of steam or a fountain. It's called the 'blow'. All whales have 'blows' of different size and shape. This can help humans to identify them when they are hidden underwater.

▶ The sperm whale is one of the greatest diving whales and may perform this sequence each time it dives to the cold, dark depths of the ocean.

1. The sperm whale surfaces and breathes in and out powerfully several times

2. It then straightens out its body and may disappear beneath the surface

▲ A giant squid tries to escape a sperm whale. The largest giant squid ever caught by a sperm whale was 12 metres in length.

Many cetaceans feed near the surface, so do not need to dive more than 50 metres down. The champion diver is the sperm whale. It can go down more than 3000 metres to hunt its prey of giant squid.

Most dolphins and porpoises dive and hold their breath for one or two minutes. Large whales can stay underwater for a longer period of time, perhaps for 15 to 20 minutes. The sperm whale can dive for more than two hours!

6. The sperm whale dives deep into the darkness of the ocean

3. The whale then reappears and begins to arch its back

4. By arching its back and tipping its head downwards, the whale prepares to dive

5. Its tail is lifted out of the water as it begins to dive

Fierce hunters

Dolphins, porpoises and toothed whales are active hunting carnivores. They eat meat – the flesh of sea creatures, especially fish and squid. Some of them crunch up hard-shelled crabs, shrimps and prawns, or shellfish, such as oysters and whelks.

A typical dolphin has 60 to 100 teeth. They are in pairs, left and right, in the upper and lower jaws. These teeth are not usually thin and sharp like fangs, but wide and cone-shaped. The teeth are the same shape all along the jaw, unlike the teeth of a cat, dog or human. This is the best design for catching their slippery food.

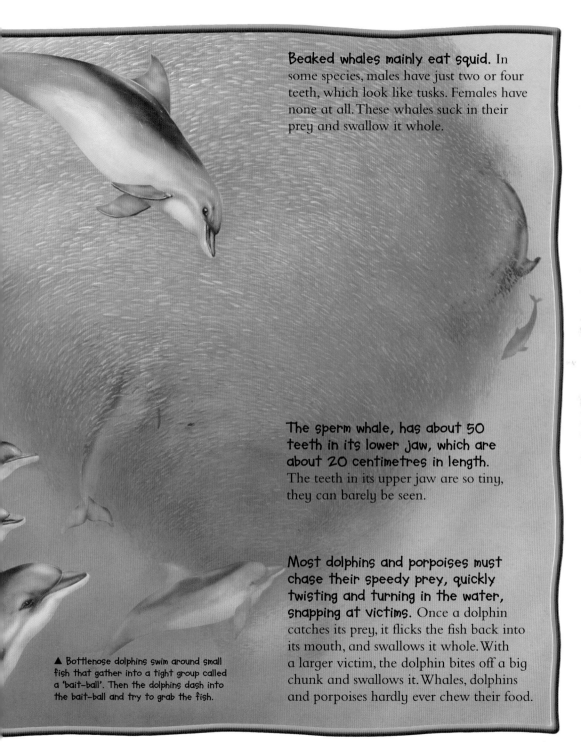

Beaked whales mainly eat squid. In some species, males have just two or four teeth, which look like tusks. Females have none at all. These whales suck in their prey and swallow it whole.

The sperm whale, has about 50 teeth in its lower jaw, which are about 20 centimetres in length. The teeth in its upper jaw are so tiny, they can barely be seen.

Most dolphins and porpoises must chase their speedy prey, quickly twisting and turning in the water, snapping at victims. Once a dolphin catches its prey, it flicks the fish back into its mouth, and swallows it whole. With a larger victim, the dolphin bites off a big chunk and swallows it. Whales, dolphins and porpoises hardly ever chew their food.

▲ Bottlenose dolphins swim around small fish that gather into a tight group called a 'bait-ball'. Then the dolphins dash into the bait-ball and try to grab the fish.

69

Sieving the sea

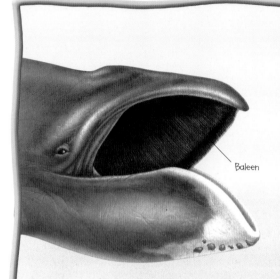

Baleen

▲ The bowhead whale's baleen hangs like a huge
curtain, big enough for ten people to hide behind.

Great whales are also called baleen whales because of the baleen in their mouths. Baleen is sometimes called whalebone, but it is not bone. It's light, tough and springy, almost like plastic. It hangs down in long strips from the whale's upper jaw. The size and shape of the strips vary from one kind of whale to another.

Most baleen whales, such as the blue, fin and sei whales, cruise-feed. This means that they feed by swimming slowly through a swarm of shrimp-like creatures called krill with their mouths open.

As a baleen whale feeds, it takes in a huge mouthful of water — enough to fill more than 100 bathtubs. This makes the skin around its throat expand like a balloon. The whale's food, such as krill, is in the water. The whale pushes the water out between the baleen plates. The baleen's bristles catch the krill like a giant filter. Then the whale licks off the krill and swallows them.

The humpback whale makes a 'bubble curtain'. It dives down, then swims up slowly in small circles as it breathes out. The bubbles created rise quickly and form a tube-shaped 'curtain' that keeps the krill or other food close together in one place as a 'bait-ball'. Then the humpback lunges into the bait-ball with its mouth wide open.

I DON'T BELIEVE IT!

In summer, the blue whale eats 4 tonnes of food in one day! That's about four million krill. In winter, it eats hardly anything for many weeks because food is scarce.

The grey whale often feeds on the shallow seabed. It swims on one side and drags its mouth through the mud. Then it pushes the water and mud out of its mouth. This traps food in its baleen, such as shellfish and shrimps. Its feeding method leaves deep grooves in the seabed, like a ploughed field.

◄ Humpback whales feed by rising up through shoals of fish with their mouths open and throat skin bulging. They scoop up water, push it out through the baleen and eat the food left inside their mouths.

71

Clicks, squeaks and squeals

Many whales, dolphins and porpoises are noisy animals. They make lots of different sounds, for various reasons. These sounds can travel long distances through the sea, so when underwater, divers can hear them. Some whale noises can be heard more than 100 kilometres away!

Sounds are made by air moving around inside the breathing passages, and also inside the intestines and stomach. In dolphins, sound waves are brought together, or focused, by the large fluid-filled lump inside the forehead called the melon. This makes sounds travel out from the front of the head in a narrow beam.

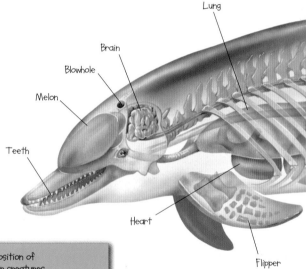

Lung

Brain

Blowhole

Melon

Teeth

Heart

Flipper

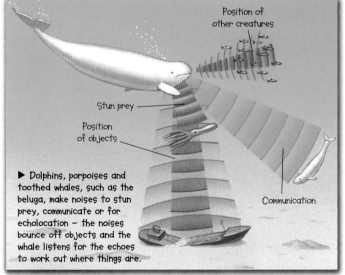

Position of other creatures

Stun prey

Position of objects

▶ Dolphins, porpoises and toothed whales, such as the beluga, make noises to stun prey, communicate or for echolocation – the noises bounce off objects and the whale listens for the echoes to work out where things are.

Communication

Sounds are especially important for detecting objects by echolocation. The dolphin detects the returning echoes of its own clicks. It can then work out the size and shape of objects nearby – whether a rock, coral, a shipwreck, an iceberg or a shoal of fish.

Sounds are also used for talking, or communication. Belugas and dolphins especially, make a vast range of clicks, squeals and squeaks. Sounds help them to stay together in their groups, and to work together as they surround a shoal of fish.

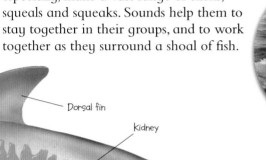

Dorsal fin

Kidney

Stomach   Intestines

Liver

Bladder

Fluke

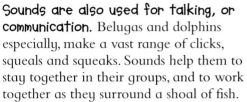

▲ To talk to each other, whales and dolphins make noises with their bodies, like slapping the surface of the water with their flukes. This is called lobtailing.

◀ Most of the inner parts of a dolphin and a human are alike, such as lungs and heart. They are also in similar positions inside the body. However, a dolphin has no hip or leg bones – and humans don't have a sound-focusing melon!

MAKE SOME DOLPHIN NOISES

You will need:
sheet of card   ruler   plastic comb

Roll the card into a funnel and squeal through the narrow end. Rub the teeth of the comb along a ruler to produce dolphin-like clicks.

Scientists have spent time closely watching dolphins to try and discover if they use a language to communicate, in the way that humans talk with words. Certain sounds seem to occur more often when dolphins are resting, swimming, playing, feeding or breeding.

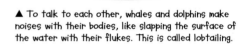

Long-distance swimmers

▲ Baleen whales, such as the humpback, travel long journeys so that they can give birth in tropical waters. Then the baby is able to grow stronger in calm waters before migrating to colder areas.

Many cetaceans migrate — go on long journeys, usually at the same time each year. This is generally to find the best food. Baleen whales spend summer in cold northern or southern waters, where there are vast amounts of food. For winter, they swim back to the tropics, where there is little food, but the waters are warm and calm.

I DON'T BELIEVE IT!
The migration of the grey whale takes less than six weeks. It would take a strong swimmer 30 weeks to complete the same journey.

Baleen whales usually swim in groups as they migrate. They can often be seen 'spyhopping'. This means they swing around into an upright position, lift their heads above the water and turn slowly to look all around as they sink back into the water. This is especially common in whales that migrate along coasts.

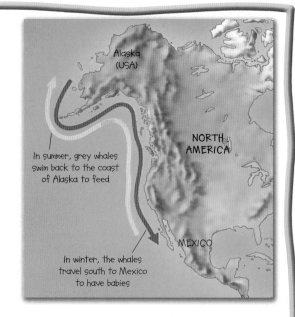

In summer, grey whales swim back to the coast of Alaska to feed

Alaska (USA)

NORTH AMERICA

MEXICO

In winter, the whales travel south to Mexico to have babies

▲ Grey whales travel up to 20,000 kilometres every year, between the icy Arctic region and warm subtropical waters.

The longest migration of any whale – and any mammal – is completed by the grey whale. In spring, grey whales swim from their breeding areas in the subtropical waters around the coast of Mexico. They head north along the west coast of North America to the Arctic Ocean for summer feeding. In autumn, they return in the opposite direction – a round trip of about 20,000 kilometres.

Many cetaceans can now be tracked by satellite. A radio beacon is fixed, usually to the dorsal fin, and its signals are picked up by satellites in space. This shows that some whales complete exactly the same migration every year, while others wander far more widely around the oceans.

Belugas and narwhals migrate from the cold waters of the southern area of the Arctic Ocean to the even icier waters further north! They follow the edge of the ice sheet as it shrinks and melts back each spring, then grows again each autumn.

◀ A tracking beacon sends out radio signals to give a whale's position every few seconds or minutes. It only works when the whale is at the surface because radio waves don't travel far through water. The batteries can last for more than two years.

Family of killers

All cetaceans are carnivores because they eat various kinds of animal as food. The killer whale can kill and eat almost any creature in the sea, from a small fish to a large whale. It is also known as the orca and is not actually a whale, but the biggest member of the dolphin family.

Killer whales live in oceans all over the world. Their black-and-white markings make them easy to recognize. Males grow up to 9 metres in length and 10 tonnes in weight. They have tall, slim, triangular fins up to 2 metres in height. Females are slightly smaller and have lower, more rounded fins.

Killer whales live in groups called pods. A pod is like a big family. Normally, there are 20 to 30 whales in a pod. Older females are usually in charge. Throughout the year, the females decide where to travel to, where to rest and when the pod will hunt.

▼ A killer whale suddenly appears out of the surf and tries to grab an unsuspecting sea lion before it has time to escape.

MAKE AN ORCA POD!

You will need:
white card   scissors   sticky tape
black pen   cotton thread

Draw and cut out killer whales of different sizes. Thread cotton through a small hole in the fin of all but the biggest whale. Then, dangle each whale from the larger whale by taping them to its body.

Members of a killer whale pod talk, or communicate, by making noises, such as clicks and grunts. They can then work together to surround a shoal of fish, such as tuna. The killer whale also feeds by 'surfing' onto a beach and grabbing a young seal or sea lion. Then the whale wriggles back into the sea, holding its victim by its sharp, back-curved teeth.

Fast and sleek

Dolphins are fast, active swimmers. They always seem to be looking for things to do, food to eat and friends to play with. They range in size from Commerson's dolphins, which are only 2 metres in length, to bottlenose dolphins, which are double the size at about 4 metres in length.

Dolphins are often seen swimming with other dolphins in large groups. Several kinds of dolphin sometimes form even bigger groups of many thousands. Pantropical spotted dolphins form huge groups and are very active – leaping and swimming. From a distance, the sea can look like it is boiling!

Many dolphins like to bow-ride. This means riding in the bow wave of a ship or boat – the v-shaped wave made by the boat's sharp front end slicing through the water. Exactly why they do this is not clear. They may be waiting for leftover food to be thrown from the boat. Or they may be saving energy by 'surfing' in the ship's wave.

▲ The Pacific white-sided dolphin is about 2 metres in length. It can often be seen riding in the bow wave of small ships and boats.

▶ Dolphins, such as these bottlenose dolphins, can often be seen leaping out of the water together.

▼ When frightened, Fraser's dolphins swim close together with lots of low leaps and splashing.

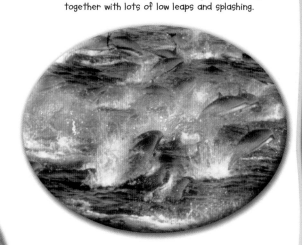

Striped dolphins are some of the fastest swimmers. They live in all oceans in groups of up to 3000. Striped dolphins often jump clear of the water in long, low leaps as they swim at speed. This is called 'porpoising', even when dolphins do it!

I DON'T BELIEVE IT!
The long tusklike tooth of the narwhal was once sold as the 'real horn' of the mythical horse, the unicorn.

Spinner dolphins are well known for their spectacular leaps high into the air. Many dolphins somersault as they leap, but spinners twist and spin around as well, five or more times in each leap. They don't seem to mind if they land on their side, tail or head, and leap out to do it again.

River dolphins

▶ As the boto comes to the surface and breathes out, the noise it produces sounds like a human sighing. Its back has a low hump rather than a dorsal fin.

Several kinds of dolphin only live in rivers or lakes. Most are rare and face many risks. They include pollution, injury from the propellers of ships, and becoming trapped in fishing nets. Other dangers include being caught as food for humans, or starvation because humans have overfished rivers and lakes.

The boto, or Amazon River dolphin, lives in several rivers in South America. It has a very long, slim, beak-like mouth and grows to about 2 metres in length. It feeds mainly in the early morning and late evening. By day it rests floating on its side, waving one flipper in the air. When the Amazon rainforest floods in the wet season, the boto swims among the huge trees, along with giant otters and piranhas.

There are three kinds of river dolphin in Asia. One is the baiji, or Yangtze dolphin of China, which has a white underside and pale blue-grey back. The others are the Indus and Ganges River dolphins, which live in Indian rivers. They are grey-brown in colour, grow to about 2 metres in length and are 80 kilograms in weight.

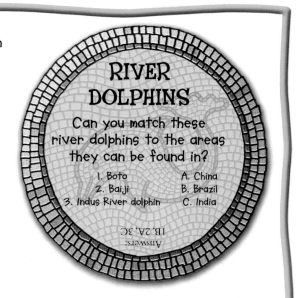

RIVER DOLPHINS

Can you match these river dolphins to the areas they can be found in?

1. Boto A. China
2. Baiji B. Brazil
3. Indus River dolphin C. India

Answers:
1B, 2A, 3C

Two kinds of dolphin live in both rivers and the sea, usually staying close to the shore. One is the tucuxi, which is quite small at just 1.5 metres in length. It can be found in the Amazon River and around the northeast coast of South America. The other is the Irrawaddy dolphin, found in the seas and rivers of Southeast Asia, from India to northern Australia. It has a blunt nose and blue-grey skin.

The franciscana or La Plata dolphin is a river dolphin that has gone back to the sea! It is similar to river dolphins, but lives in shallow water along the southeast coasts of South America. It can be recognized by its very long, slim, sword-like beak.

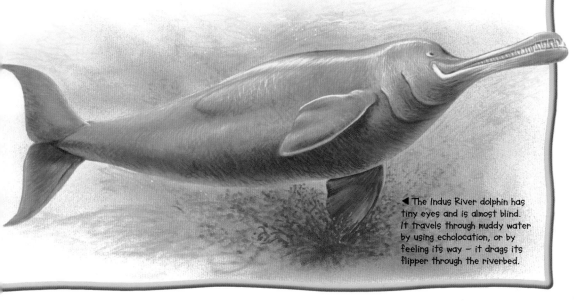

◀ The Indus River dolphin has tiny eyes and is almost blind. It travels through muddy water by using echolocation, or by feeling its way – it drags its flipper through the riverbed.

Shy and secretive

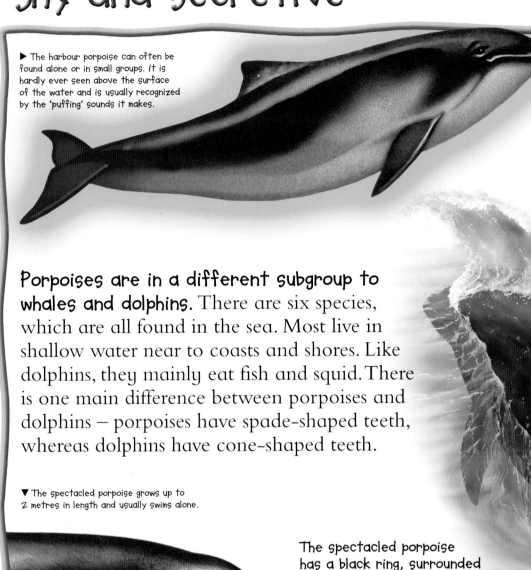

▶ The harbour porpoise can often be found alone or in small groups. It is hardly ever seen above the surface of the water and is usually recognized by the 'puffing' sounds it makes.

Porpoises are in a different subgroup to whales and dolphins. There are six species, which are all found in the sea. Most live in shallow water near to coasts and shores. Like dolphins, they mainly eat fish and squid. There is one main difference between porpoises and dolphins – porpoises have spade-shaped teeth, whereas dolphins have cone-shaped teeth.

▼ The spectacled porpoise grows up to 2 metres in length and usually swims alone.

The spectacled porpoise has a black ring, surrounded by a white ring, around each eye. It can be found in the Southern Ocean around the lower tip of South America, and near islands such as the Falklands and South Georgia. It has a very striking pattern – its top half is black and its lower half is white!

The harbour or common porpoise is familiar to sailors around the northern waters. It has the nickname 'puffing pig' because its blow is rarely seen, but can be heard as a series of loud, short puffs – like a mixture of a snort and a sneeze. It eats a wide range of food, including leftovers thrown from boats.

STRANDED!

You're at the beach and you see a stranded whale, do you...

A. Run away and keep quiet
B. Find an adult, and contact the police or coastguard
C. Sing the whale a song

Answer: B

Dall's porpoise is the largest of the group, at about 2 metres in length and 200 kilograms in weight. It lives along the shores of the North Pacific Ocean. It's a fast and agile swimmer, dashing along at over 50 kilometres an hour. However, it rarely leaps above the surface of the water like other porpoises.

▲ When Dall's porpoise swims quickly through water, a long, narrow spray spurts along its back. It is known as the 'rooster's tail' due to its shape.

83

Getting together

Whales, dolphins and porpoises breed like most other mammals. A male and female get together and mate. The female become pregnant and a baby develops inside her womb. The baby is born through her birth canal, which is a small opening near her tail.

Breeding narwhals can be dangerous. This is because the males swipe and jab each other with their long 'tusks' to try and become partners for waiting females. The tusk is a very long left upper tooth that grows like a sword with a corkscrew pattern. Usually only the males have a tusk, which can be up to 3 metres in length.

◀ At breeding time male narwhals 'fence' with their tusks. They're competing for a female.

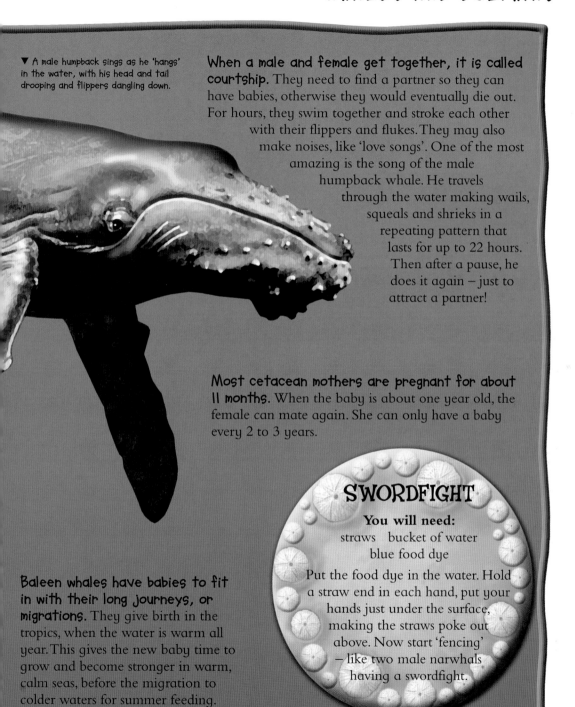

▼ A male humpback sings as he 'hangs' in the water, with his head and tail drooping and flippers dangling down.

When a male and female get together, it is called courtship. They need to find a partner so they can have babies, otherwise they would eventually die out. For hours, they swim together and stroke each other with their flippers and flukes. They may also make noises, like 'love songs'. One of the most amazing is the song of the male humpback whale. He travels through the water making wails, squeals and shrieks in a repeating pattern that lasts for up to 22 hours. Then after a pause, he does it again – just to attract a partner!

Most cetacean mothers are pregnant for about 11 months. When the baby is about one year old, the female can mate again. She can only have a baby every 2 to 3 years.

Baleen whales have babies to fit in with their long journeys, or migrations. They give birth in the tropics, when the water is warm all year. This gives the new baby time to grow and become stronger in warm, calm seas, before the migration to colder waters for summer feeding.

SWORDFIGHT

You will need:
straws   bucket of water
blue food dye

Put the food dye in the water. Hold a straw end in each hand, put your hands just under the surface, making the straws poke out above. Now start 'fencing' – like two male narwhals having a swordfight.

Baby whales and dolphins

Most whale, dolphin and porpoise mothers have one baby at a time. Twins or more are very rare. The baby, called a calf, is usually born tail first. It needs to start breathing air at once. The mother nudges it up to the surface of the water, so it can gasp its first breaths.

A new baby stays very close to its mother. She protects it, charging at enemies, such as sharks, large sea lions and seals – and perhaps killer whales.

Like other mammals, the mother feeds her baby on her own milk. It is very rich and full of goodness. The calf sucks it from the mother's teat, which is usually hidden under a fold of skin on her underside.

◄ The young beluga is born dark grey or pinky-grey. It gradually becomes lighter, but it may not take on its all-white colouration until it is more than five years old.

Most baby cetaceans feed on their mother's milk for about one year. They grow quickly and soon become strong swimmers. Their mothers teach them how to hunt. By 18 to 24 months of age, the young are independent – able to look after themselves. Baby baleen whales feed on their mother's milk for less time, for only 6 to 8 months.

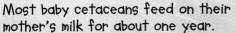

I DON'T BELIEVE IT!

The blue whale is the world's biggest baby at 7 metres in length and 3 tonnes in weight. It drinks 350 litres of its mother's milk everyday – enough to fill four bathtubs!

It is difficult to know how long whales, dolphins and porpoises live. Scientists can guess their age from the way their teeth grow. Inside the teeth of some species are rings, like the rings in tree trunks. On average, there is one ring for each year of growth. Most dolphins survive for 5 to 25 years. Baleen whales may live for 70 to 80 years. However, some whales and dolphins have been known to survive much longer.

◄ Some baby whales and dolphins, such as this young striped dolphin, have different colours and patterns to the adults. Their colours change as they grow older.

Harm and help

▶ Pilot whales can be found in groups. This makes it easier for whale hunters to catch them.

I DON'T BELIEVE IT!
There are stories of people being saved by dolphins when in danger at sea. The dolphin may nudge them to shore. Some people even tell of dolphins protecting them from sharks!

Most baleen whales are protected by law around the world. Only a small amount of controlled hunting is allowed, although illegal hunting continues in some countries. Conservation parks, such as the Southern Sanctuary in Antarctica, are set aside to protect marine life.

However, hunting still goes on. Not only of large whales, but also of smaller whales, dolphins and porpoises. Some whalers have turned to catching smaller types, such as melon-headed whales and pilot whales. If the hunting continues, they may also face extinction.

Whales and dolphins can drown even though they live in water. If they get stuck underwater for some reason, they cannot breathe and may die. One of the greatest dangers for cetaceans is becoming trapped in fishing nets – this causes nearly 1000 to die each day.

Another hazard is pollution. Chemicals from coastal factories, power stations and oil refineries wash along rivers into the sea. Some dolphins – especially river dolphins – and porpoises are badly affected because they live near the shore.

Ecotourism is becoming popular – seeing wildlife in its natural setting, while hardly disturbing it. People take trips on whale-watching boats, or swim with dolphins near the beach. The money made should be used to support wildlife and conservation. In some places this does not happen, and the whales and dolphins are disturbed or frightened. It's a delicate balance between our use of the sea and its creatures, and looking after their environment and well-being.

▼ Bottlenose dolphins soon learn to take food from divers, but this may affect their natural behaviour and their ability to survive.

89

Penguins

Take a journey to the coldest, emptiest places on Earth to meet these fascinating flightless birds.

Antarctica • Flippers and feet • Swimming • Diving
Emperors • Communication • Gentoos and Chinstraps
Jackass penguins • Chicks • Predators • Feeding
King penguins • Adelie penguins • Rookeries

Bold, beautiful birds

Penguins are peculiar birds unlike any others on the planet. They have feathers that are more like fur, and wings that are more like flippers. Penguins live in some of the coldest, windiest and emptiest locations, yet they are still some of the most recognizable birds on Earth.

▶ Penguins, such as these king penguins, are fascinating flightless birds that live extraordinary lives. They are unlike any other type of animal in appearance, and they face incredible challenges to survive from day to day.

What is a penguin?

Like all birds, penguins are covered in feathers and lay eggs. Most birds have bodies that help them fly, but penguins' bodies are perfectly suited to swimming. There are 17 types of penguin, all quite similar in appearance.

Penguins have stout, upright bodies covered in black-and-white feathers. Their black backs and white bellies help to camouflage the birds as they swim. When seen from below penguins appear white, blending into the light sky, but when seen from above they blend into the dark sea water.

▶ Birds, like this Chinstrap penguin, are vertebrates — just like reptiles, amphibians and mammals. This means that they have bony skeletons that support their bodies.

Skull

Spine

Bill (beak)

The bones in a penguin's flipper are similar to those in other birds' wings, and a human's arm

Ribcage

Hip bone

Penguins have sharp-clawed toes on their feet

◀ Penguins evolved (gradually changed over millions of years) from flying birds into flightless birds, so their flippers look quite similar to wings.

All birds have wings, but not all of them can fly. Wings are limbs, just like arms and legs, but they are mostly used for flying. The wings of penguins are too small and stumpy to be used for flight, but they have evolved for moving through water.

Flipper of a
Magellanic penguin

Wing of a
herring gull

▼ The long-extinct *Waimanu* had bird-like wings, rather than flippers, but probably could not fly.

The largest penguin that ever lived was almost as tall as a human. Scientists know this from studying fossil bones of penguins that lived millions of years ago. These bones give us clues about how prehistoric penguins looked and behaved. *Waimanu*, for example, was a small penguin-like bird that lived around 60 million years ago.

Male and female penguins usually look alike. It is very difficult to tell them apart, but the males are often taller and slightly heavier. Most penguins build nests or dig burrows where they lay their eggs, and both parents help to take care of the eggs and chicks.

Creature features

The body of a penguin is perfectly suited to life in the water, rather than life in the air. The ancestors of penguins were probably flying birds, but at some point in the past their bodies evolved to make them swim faster and better, and they lost their flight feathers. They dive into water to catch sea animals such as fish, so penguins can eat food that few other birds can reach.

Penguins are the only flightless waterbirds. Other flightless birds, such as ostriches, emus and rheas are fast runners on land. They are far too heavy to fly, but can outrun most of their predators. Like penguins, they make their nests on the ground rather than in trees.

▼ Most birds have hollow bones so they can fly. Penguins, such as this Galapagos penguin, have solid bones so they can dive underwater without floating to the surface.

Flying away

Penguins can't fly, but there are plenty of other unusual animals that can soar through the air. Do some research, and find out information on:

1. Flying lemurs
2. Flying squirrels
3. Flying lizards
4. Flying fish

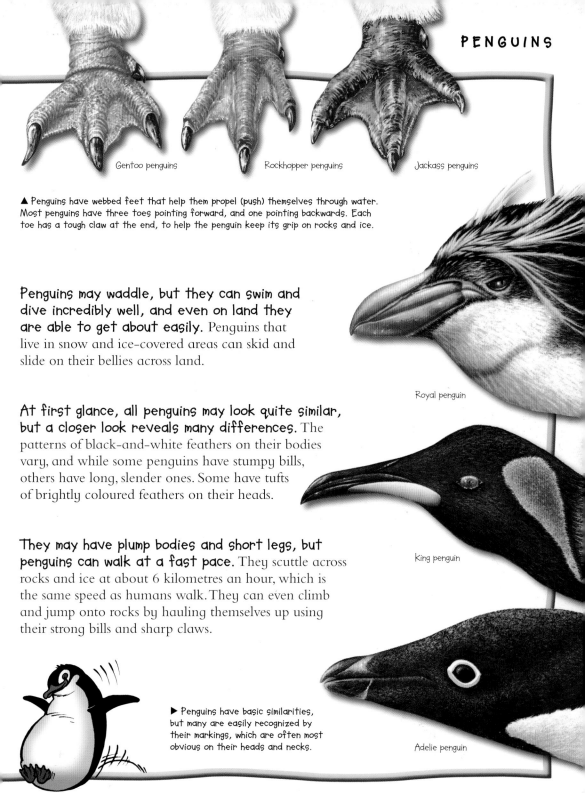

Gentoo penguins   Rockhopper penguins   Jackass penguins

▲ Penguins have webbed feet that help them propel (push) themselves through water. Most penguins have three toes pointing forward, and one pointing backwards. Each toe has a tough claw at the end, to help the penguin keep its grip on rocks and ice.

Penguins may waddle, but they can swim and dive incredibly well, and even on land they are able to get about easily. Penguins that live in snow and ice-covered areas can skid and slide on their bellies across land.

Royal penguin

At first glance, all penguins may look quite similar, but a closer look reveals many differences. The patterns of black-and-white feathers on their bodies vary, and while some penguins have stumpy bills, others have long, slender ones. Some have tufts of brightly coloured feathers on their heads.

They may have plump bodies and short legs, but penguins can walk at a fast pace. They scuttle across rocks and ice at about 6 kilometres an hour, which is the same speed as humans walk. They can even climb and jump onto rocks by hauling themselves up using their strong bills and sharp claws.

King penguin

▶ Penguins have basic similarities, but many are easily recognized by their markings, which are often most obvious on their heads and necks.

Adelie penguin

97

On the ice

Penguins live in the Southern Hemisphere. This is the half of the Earth below the Equator (the imaginary line that runs through the middle of the Earth). Antarctica and the South Pole are found here, and many types of penguin make this icy habitat their home.

It is easier to stay warm if you have a bigger body. For this reason, the biggest penguins normally live in the coldest regions, and the smallest penguins live in warmer places.

▼ These eight species (types) of penguin live in or around the freezing Antarctic – the coldest, driest and windiest place on Earth.

In the Antarctic, winter temperatures drop as low as −70°C. The land is covered in ice, and penguins that live here battle against the worst weather on Earth.

King

Adelie

Rockhopper

The largest penguins are Emperor penguins.
They measure just over one metre in height,
and weigh up to 40 kilograms. Their bulk helps
them to keep warm in temperatures that reach
far below zero.

Emperor

▶ The shaded areas on
the map show where these
penguins may be found.

SOUTH
AMERICA

ATLANTIC
OCEAN

AFRICA

INDIAN
OCEAN

PACIFIC
OCEAN

ANTARCTICA

NEW
ZEALAND

AUSTRALIA

Gentoo

Royal

**There is a layer of ice 4 kilometres
deep covering the Antarctic, and it
is so cold even the sea freezes over.**
During the winter there may only be
sunlight for an hour a day, but in the
middle of summer daylight lasts for
nearly 24 hours.

Chinstrap

Macaroni

Getting warmer

Not all penguins are found in cold places – some live in areas where the weather can be very hot. These birds are found in places, such as South America, Australia, New Zealand and South Africa, or even on islands at the Equator, where the temperatures can soar.

Penguins that live in warm places often get too hot. Some of them have patches of bare skin on their faces to help them stay cool. If they get too hot, they may rest in burrows, or leap into the sea.

The air may be warm, but the sea is still cold. Currents from the Antarctic bring chilly water to the coastal areas where these penguins hunt for fish and other food. They have to be able to survive both hot and cold temperatures.

Peruvian

Snares

Little

Fjordland

Magellanic

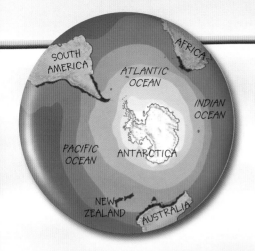

Most penguins live in remote places where there are few other animals. They are not used to defending themselves against predators, such as wild dogs and cats, so they find it difficult to survive anywhere these animals live.

Little penguins of Australia and New Zealand often live near people's homes along the shore. They are shy birds, but often build their nests beneath beach houses. These are the smallest penguins, measuring only 35 centimetres in height.

▲▼ These nine species of penguin, live in the Southern Hemisphere, some distance from the ice-covered South Pole. The shaded areas on the map show where these penguins live.

Erect-crested

Jackass

Galapagos

Yellow-eyed

Life below zero

Animals that live in icy places have bodies that can keep heat in and cold out. Penguins that live in, or near, Antarctica have feathers that lie close to their bodies when they are in the sea, locking out water. When on land, the feathers trap warm air close to the penguins' bodies. On warm days, penguins ruffle their feathers so that warm air escapes.

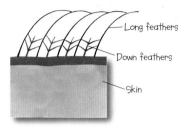

1. Long feathers overlap, trapping warm air next to the skin

Long feathers
Down feathers
Skin

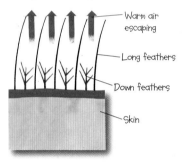

2. Long feathers separate, letting warm air escape

Warm air escaping
Long feathers
Down feathers
Skin

▲ A layer of short feathers lie next to a penguin's skin. The longer top feathers overlap to trap warm air, or separate to allow it to escape.

Penguins make an oily substance in a special place near their tails. They spread this over their feathers with their bills and this helps to keep water away from their skin. When penguins clean the dirt from their feathers and coat them with oil they are said to be 'preening'.

◀ This king penguin is using oil from the gland at the base of its tail to preen its feathers.

▲ Emperor penguin chicks sit on their parents' feet to keep from freezing to death on the snow-covered ground.

A thick layer of fat (blubber) keeps penguins warm. The blubber may be several centimetres thick. Other animals that live in the oceans, such as whales, also have blubber under their skin. Substances that keep in the warmth, such as blubber, are called 'insulators'.

Penguins sometimes sunbathe to help warm up their bodies. The black feathers on their backs absorb sunlight and pass the heat to the penguins' skin. Penguins that live in the Antarctic can even get too hot, and have to take a dip in the sea to cool down!

Penguin chicks can easily freeze to death. Parent birds stay with their chicks while they are young, and hold them next to their bodies. This is called brooding and it means that the warmth from the body of the parent is passed to the chick, keeping it warm and dry until it grows its own waterproof feathers.

I DON'T BELIEVE IT!

Few fish-eating animals live around the Antarctic, so there is plenty of food for those animals, such as penguins, that can cope with extreme temperatures and winds.

Swimmers and divers

▼ As it swims, the Chinstrap's head, body, legs and tail all make one smooth shape, which glides easily through the water.

Penguins may look clumsy on land, but they move gracefully through the oceans. While other water birds, such as ducks and geese, swim on the top of water, penguins can dive deep below the surface as they hunt for food. Some penguins can swim at speeds of 14 kilometres an hour for short periods of time.

Animals that move through water at speed have bodies that are shaped like bullets. This body shape is said to be 'streamlined' – meaning that it can move smoothly through water. Whales, dolphins, fish and seals also have streamlined bodies.

Fish breathe underwater, but penguins need to come to the surface for air. This means that, no matter how deep or far they swim, they need to put their heads above water to breathe. Some penguins can only stay underwater for a minute or two, but Emperor penguins can dive for 18 minutes at a time and can swim to depths of over 500 metres.

▶ Emperor penguins have highly streamlined bodies and excellent underwater vision, allowing them to dive to incredible depths when they hunt.

Penguins use their flippers to move through water, and their webbed feet to change direction. When penguins swim on the surface of water they use their flippers like oars.

▲ It takes a lot of strength and power for an Emperor penguin to push its large body out of the water and leap on to land.

Swimming penguins leap out of water for a few metres, before diving back in. This is called 'porpoising' (after porpoises, which do this frequently) and it means a penguin can grab a lungful of air without slowing down. This is especially useful when chasing prey, or trying to escape a predator.

I DON'T BELIEVE IT!

Penguins have excellent vision and can swim to depths where there is little or no light. It's possible that penguins also use other senses to find prey in the dark, but no one knows for sure.

King penguins

▼ Adult King penguins breed on the rocky islands in and around the Antarctic.

King penguins are unusually colourful, with bold orange and gold patches of plumage. They are the second largest type of penguin, reaching about 90 centimetres in height. Kings live on islands in the Southern Hemisphere, near the fringes of the Antarctic region. When on land, they have to cope with cold, windy weather.

When it is time to breed, King penguins settle on flat land close to the sea. They don't make nests, and the females lay just one egg each year, which is unusual for penguins. The males protect the eggs by holding them on their feet, tucked under the warm fur on their bellies. Keeping the eggs off the ground prevents them from freezing.

Living in a group helps penguins keep warm. Huge groups (colonies) of King penguins huddle together at breeding time. There may be as many as 10,000 birds in a single huddle.

Chicks stay with their parents for about a year before they are ready to survive on their own. Chicks rely on their parents to bring them food, and some chicks have been known to survive for several months without eating.

King penguins mostly eat squid and lanternfish. Lanternfish have an unusual ability to make light in their bodies. The bright flashes of light help the shoal, or group, of lanternfish stick together as they swim through the dark ocean depths, but it also helps King penguins find them too.

▼ King penguin chicks are covered in downy feathers until they are about 10 months old, when they grow adult feathers. The downy feathers fall out, or moult, as the new plumage grows.

▲ Chicks have lots of body fat to keep them warm and provide them with energy while they are waiting for food from their parents. The fat is turned into sugar inside their bodies, and this keeps them alive.

I DON'T BELIEVE IT!

Penguins can take a nap at almost any time, anywhere. They mostly sleep at night, but can doze sitting, standing, lying down or even while swimming.

107

Adelie penguins

Adelie penguins are plain-looking birds. They have black coats, white bellies and black heads with white rings around their eyes. Their pointed tails drag behind them as they walk across the Antarctic snow and ice.

▼ Like their close relatives, the Gentoo and Chinstrap penguins, Adelies have long tail feathers that brush the snow as they walk.

▼ Adult Adelies are about 70 centimetres tall and weigh around 5.5 kilograms. They are small, but they are strong swimmers and leapers.

Adelies live in one of the harshest places on Earth, but they are great survivors. Around five million adult Adelies live in the Antarctic, often in huge groups that number tens of thousands.

Pebbles are very valuable to an Adelie penguin. They use them to make their nests, which may also contain bones and moss. Fights often break out over pebbles, with neighbours often stealing the best ones!

A female lays two eggs, and then leaves to hunt in the sea. The male guards the eggs and keeps them warm. If he leaves them they will freeze and the growing chick will die. When the female returns, 10 to 14 days later, the parents take turns to guard the eggs.

▲ Large seabirds will sometimes try to steal food from adult Adelies as they are feeding their chicks.

I DON'T BELIEVE IT!

Adelie penguin parents sometimes have to travel up to 120 kilometres in search of food to feed their chicks.

Parades of Adelie penguins march towards the edge of the ice. They have to walk from the colony, where their nests are, to the sea, where they can catch food. Once at the water's edge they look out for predators, such as leopard seals, before leaping into the water.

Life in a rookery

Penguins are sociable animals and they like to live in large groups. They come together, often in their thousands, when it is time to breed. The large groups they form are called rookeries.

Different types of penguin live in rookeries at different times of year — it all depends on when they breed. Little penguins come ashore in May or June to start mating. They may produce one, two or even three broods (clutches of eggs) through the breeding season. King penguins make their rookeries in October and November.

▶ A rookery only contains one type, or species, of penguin. These are King penguins. Rookeries are made up of lots of families that are related to one another.

The largest rookeries may have several million penguins in them. Penguins stay in their rookery during the whole breeding season, leaving only to look for food. For this reason, most rookeries occur in coastal areas, near water. When looking for food, they often stay in small groups and hunt together.

Living in groups helps penguins to stay warm and safe. When the wind blows and the temperature drops far below zero, penguins huddle together for warmth. Huddling also helps to protect the eggs and chicks from predators, especially gulls and other sea birds.

Rookeries are noisy, busy, smelly places. Thousands, or millions, of penguins call to each other constantly. Their waste (called guano) builds up, and some penguins use it as a building material when constructing their nests.

Emperors

The biggest species (type) of penguin is the Emperor. Along with Kings, they are known as the 'great penguins' and are probably most closely related to the prehistoric giant penguins. They feed mainly on squid, fish and krill – small marine animals similar to shrimps.

▼ Webbed feet and flippers help penguins, such as these emperors, keep their balance on slippery ice, but it's not unusual for them to topple over and start tobogganing on their fronts!

All Emperors live and breed in the Antarctic. Their bodies are adapted for the incredibly cold weather, and they have feathers on their legs all the way down to their feet. There are about 40 breeding colonies of Emperors in the Antarctic, and each colony can have more than 100,000 adults.

When these penguins breed they have to face an extraordinary test of strength and endurance. In March the adults come ashore and walk for up to 200 kilometres to reach their breeding ground. The female lays a single egg, which the male immediately scoops on to his feet, where it is kept warm and safe by a thick flap of skin on his belly.

While the females walk all the way back to the sea to hunt for food, the males huddle together and look after their eggs. They have to wait for nine weeks until the females return – and during this time they survive without any food at all. While the males are waiting they have to cope with hurricane-force winds and some of the coldest temperatures on Earth.

On their return, the females take over the care of the chicks, and the males return to the sea to hunt. The females regurgitate food (bring food back up into their mouths) to feed the chicks. Through the rest of the winter the parents take it in turns to keep the growing chick warm and fetch food from the sea.

I DON'T BELIEVE IT!

A male Emperor penguin goes without food for up to 115 days while it courts, mates, incubates its egg and looks after its chick. During this time it can lose up to one-third of its body weight.

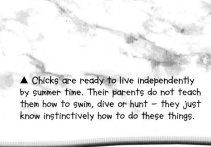

▲ Chicks are ready to live independently by summer time. Their parents do not teach them how to swim, dive or hunt – they just know instinctively how to do these things.

Say and display

All animals communicate with each other, and voices and body language are two of the most important ways. Penguins often communicate by calling to each other. The type of calls depend on the species of penguin, and what message they want to get across.

◄ Chinstrap penguins put on a display to impress potential mates. They bob their heads up and down and make a great deal of noise, sounding like braying donkeys or hissing cats.

Penguins use body language to choose a mate. When males want to attract a female they stand tall with their necks outstretched, bray loudly and spread their flippers wide. Interested females copy the males and raise their heads, stretching tall.

QUIZ

Which of the examples of body language listed below will a penguin use to attract a mate?

1. Standing tall
2. Spreading their flippers wide
3. Making loud braying noises

Answer:
All are true.

◀ Male Gentoo penguins offer their females pebbles for building a large nest, which will protect their two eggs.

When an adult penguin returns from the sea it can't rely on sight alone to find its chick. Penguins sometimes have their own 'meeting places' where members of the family go to find one another. Adults can recognize the screech of their own chicks, even when thousands of other chicks are calling at the same time.

Gentoo penguins value pebbles, which they use to build their nests. Males sometimes give their mates pebbles as a gift. Penguins steal nesting materials, such as pebbles and plants, from one another's nests and this can cause fights.

Adelie penguins defend their territories fiercely. They use body language – such as pointing with their flippers and staring – to scare others away. If their warnings aren't heeded they attack the other animal, beating them with their flippers.

▼ Royal penguins often squabble over nesting spaces and these fights can result in eggs being crushed.

115

Gentoos and Chinstraps

Gentoos have bright-orange bills and feet. Their feathers are black and white, with white patches above their eyes. Gentoos gather in large groups when they nest. They lay two eggs in September or October and the chicks hatch 34 days later. Both parents share the task of feeding the chicks.

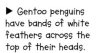
▶ Gentoo penguins have bands of white feathers across the top of their heads.

Adult penguins moult (lose their feathers) when their youngsters become independent. During moulting, which takes place once a year, a penguin sheds its damaged or old feathers so new ones can replace them. A moulting penguin looks strange, as new feathers force the old ones out. Moulting takes several weeks, and during this time an adult penguin can't go into the sea because its plumage is not waterproof.

◀ Moulting adult penguins have to go without food until their new plumage grows. Before moulting, penguins increase the amount they eat to build stores of fat in their bodies.

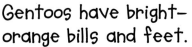

There are around 12 million Chinstraps. These medium-sized penguins have black-and-white feathers. Chinstraps can be recognized by the distinctive narrow band of black feathers that run from one side of their heads to the other, under their bills. This makes them look as if they are wearing helmets, which are strapped on under their chins, and gives them their name.

▼ Chinstrap penguins live in cold, bleak places. When climbing over rocks and ice they sometimes use all four limbs, and they are able to jump long distances.

I DON'T BELIEVE IT!

Chinstraps can be very aggressive, and will beat each other with their stumpy wings or bite hard. They will even attack humans if they come into contact with them.

Chinstraps and Gentoos live near the Antarctic. They swim in freezing water, searching for tiny marine animals and fish to eat. When they come to land they often huddle together on massive ice floes.

Chilly chicks

Life for a penguin chick is very tough, and many never make it to adulthood. Female penguins normally lay two eggs, but often only one survives. The first chick hatches from its egg several days before the second, and gets a head start. By the time the second chick emerges, the first chick is much bigger and stronger, and is more likely to be fed by its parents.

Young chicks are covered in fluffy feathers, and they look nothing like their parents for some time. The feathers are not good at keeping heat in, but they allow the heat from the body of an adult penguin to get to the chick's skin. Chicks that live in very cold places may easily freeze to death, especially if their parents get so hungry they have to desert them to feed.

Chicks huddle together in groups when their parents leave them. These groups are called nurseries, or crèches, and a few adult penguins usually stay behind to protect the youngsters from predators.

◄ These Emperor chicks are huddling together for warmth. They rely on their parents until they have grown thicker layers of waterproof feathers. When they have grown their first adult plumage, chicks are known as fledglings.

Penguin chicks can survive for days without food, unlike the chicks of other birds. As it gets older, a chick's parents may disappear for days, or weeks at a time, hunting for food in the ocean. Thanks to their thick layers of fat, penguin chicks do not starve to death during this time. Birds that fly can't have large stores of fat, or they would never get off the ground!

► Some penguins, like this Gentoo, lay two eggs. Only one chick will survive unless the parents can find enough food for both.

South American penguins

Some penguins never see snow and can suffer from too much heat! These warm-weather penguins have to shelter from the hot sun, rather than the polar winds of the South Pole. They do not need so many layers of fat to keep them warm, so they are thinner than the penguins of Antarctica.

Almost 500 years ago, an explorer from Portugal came to South America and thought he'd found a new type of flightless goose. The man was called Ferdinand Magellan and he gave his name to these new birds – Magellanic penguins. Sadly Magellan and his crewmates were not very interested in the birds, except as a source of food.

Magellanic penguins live around the coast of South America and nearby islands. When they come to land to breed they choose large, flat, sandy or pebbly places to build their nests and often share their nesting grounds with sea lions. Although the sea lions rarely eat the penguins, they often attack them.

▼ Magellanic penguins lay their eggs in burrows, which they dig near bushes, shrubs or grass so that they can shelter from the wind and sun.

▲ Peruvian penguins lay their eggs in burrows dug out of guano (their waste), which has built up over many centuries.

Galapagos penguins live further north than any other penguins. They make their homes on the Galapagos Islands, which lie off the west coast of South America and cross the Equator. Here the temperatures soar and the sun is very strong. To try and keep cool these little penguins hunt for fish and squid during the day and only come on to land at night.

Peruvian penguins live on the desert coasts of Peru and Chile, in South America. Like Galapagos and Magellanic penguins, they make burrows to protect their eggs and chicks, although they sometimes build nests in caves or under rocks. They are very shy birds, and avoid humans.

◀ Peruvian penguins have a thick black bar of feathers across their front. They are sometimes called Humboldts, which is the name of a current of cold water that flows along the South American coast.

Penguin predators

A predator is an animal that preys on (hunts) other animals to eat. Penguins mainly live in places where there are few predators. When they dive into the ocean, penguins need to stay alert, as there are sea-living predators such as sharks, seals and whales that may hunt them.

Penguin eggs make tasty food for many different animals. Parent birds sometimes have to leave their eggs or chicks unprotected. At these times hungry predators, such as skuas and gulls, will try and grab them.

Penguins on land may be attacked by wild animals. In Antarctica, penguins have little to fear from other animals as few creatures can survive in this barren habitat. Elsewhere, however, nesting penguins are easy prey for cats, dogs, foxes and ferrets, and if they see one of these predators approaching they head for the water quickly.

Leopard seals and sea lions attack penguins when they swim and dive. These big animals spend most of their lives in water, but come to the surface to breathe. Some of them can stay underwater for more than an hour at a time and can dive to depths of 100 metres. Penguins are the leopard seal's main source of food.

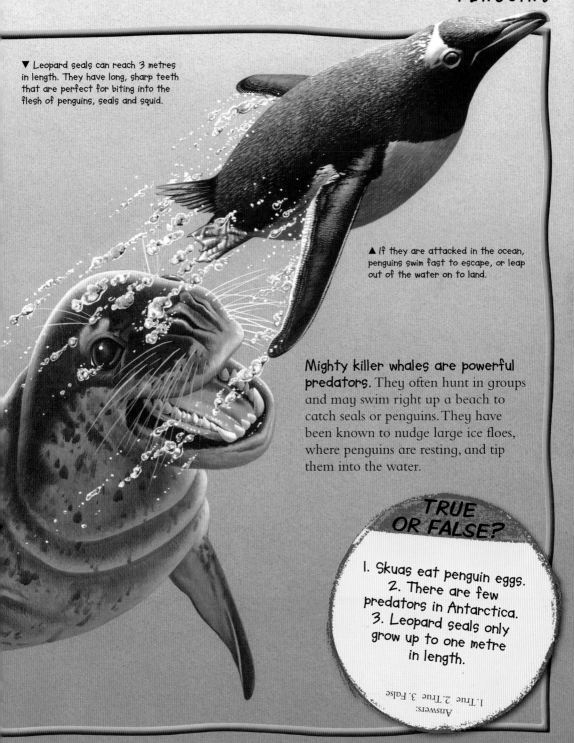

▼ Leopard seals can reach 3 metres in length. They have long, sharp teeth that are perfect for biting into the flesh of penguins, seals and squid.

▲ If they are attacked in the ocean, penguins swim fast to escape, or leap out of the water on to land.

Mighty killer whales are powerful predators. They often hunt in groups and may swim right up a beach to catch seals or penguins. They have been known to nudge large ice floes, where penguins are resting, and tip them into the water.

TRUE OR FALSE?

1. Skuas eat penguin eggs.
2. There are few predators in Antarctica.
3. Leopard seals only grow up to one metre in length.

Answers:
1. True 2. True 3. False

Jackass penguins

Jackass penguins get their name from their loud, braying call, which sounds like a donkey, or jackass. They are also known as African or Black-footed penguins. Jackass penguins reach about 60 centimetres in height and live on the coasts of South Africa and nearby islands.

Only a few hundred years ago there were millions of Jackass penguins living in South Africa. Now there are only 50,000 breeding pairs. Many have been killed by hunters, or have lost their habitats. Now they are protected, but they remain in danger of extinction (dying out).

▲ Jackass penguins are popular with tourists in South Africa, who enjoy watching these tame and friendly birds.

TRUE OR FALSE?

1. Emperor penguins live in Australia.
2. Penguins can breathe underwater.
3. Kiwis are also flightless birds.
4. The Antarctic is at the South Pole.

Answers:
3 and 4 are true.

Jackasses build their burrows in guano.
Huge piles of bird waste covered many
coasts and islands for hundreds of years,
until Europeans began to remove it to use
as fertilizer (a substance that is dug into soil
to help plants grow). Without the guano,
the penguins couldn't protect their eggs
and chicks. Now local people and tourists
are giving them ready-made burrows.

▲ While some penguins use pebbles to build
their nests, Jackass penguins favour twigs.

**If the weather gets too hot,
Jackass penguins leave their
nests and return to the cool
water.** These hot days sometimes
happen at the beginning of a
nesting season, when some
penguins have already laid
their eggs. The parents may
not return for six weeks,
and by then their eggs
will have been eaten
by sea birds.

**Females lay their eggs throughout the
year.** Usually two eggs are laid at a time,
and they are cared for by both parents,
who may stay together for life. The eggs
are incubated (kept warm) for about
40 days before hatching.

Dinner time

Penguins are active birds, and they need to eat a lot of food to give them energy. Most penguins survive on a mixed diet of fish, squid and crustaceans, such as crabs and krill. Adelie penguins feed on krill, and can eat up to one kilogram every day.

Penguins have a clever way of providing food for their youngsters. When adult penguins catch food for their chicks they have to carry it – firstly as they swim through the ocean – and then as they walk to their breeding grounds. They do this by means of a special stomach-like pouch, called a crop, in their throats. The food can stay in the crop for several days.

▶ Young penguins, like this Chinstrap chick, peck at an adult's mouth to encourage them to regurgitate their food. Chicks pester any passing adult for food, not just their parents!

Parent birds feed their chicks by regurgitating the food from their crops. Food passes from the parent's crop to its bill, and then into a chick's open mouth. Most penguins live near the sea, so they are never far from food, but Emperor penguins sometimes have to travel over 1000 kilometres in a single hunting trip. They can carry more than 4 kilograms of food in their crops.

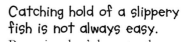

QUIZ
1. How much krill can Adelie penguins eat in a day?
2. What is the name of the stomach-like pouch in a penguin's throat?
3. Do penguins have teeth?

Answers:
1. One kilogram 2. Crop 3. No

Catching hold of a slippery fish is not always easy. Penguins don't have teeth so they swallow their food whole. Their bills have sharp edges that can grip a fish or squid tightly.

Seas and oceans may be teeming with life in some areas, but rather empty in others. This is because the oceans of the world are greatly affected by warm and cold currents of water that flow through them. The currents change during the seasons, and over many years. Places with cool currents often have more food than those with warm currents, so this is where penguins hunt.

▶ Spikes inside their mouths and spines on their tongues help penguins, like this Jackass, keep hold of their prey until they can swallow it.

Crested clowns

▲ Rockhoppers bounce from boulder to boulder. They are aggressive, noisy birds.

The six species of crested penguins have decorative head feathers. Rockhoppers are one of the most familiar crested penguins, and the smallest. They are found mainly on islands in the subantarctic region where there are no beaches and they have to slip, slide and jump into the water. To get back on land they leap straight out of the sea.

Fjordland penguins of New Zealand are so shy that little is known about them. They hide in their nests at the foot of trees or in sheltered areas of forests where they live. Scientists fear that few of these penguins are left, and they may become extinct.

Snares penguins live only on Snares Islands near New Zealand and their habitat is protected. People are rarely allowed on the islands, which are covered in trees and plants. The penguins make their rookeries in the forests.

I DON'T BELIEVE IT!

Macaroni penguins were named after British men in the 18th century who dressed up in fancy clothes and were known as 'macaronis'.

▲ Erect-crested penguins are closely related to Snares and Fjordland penguins.

Crested penguins usually lay two eggs. Only one is likely to hatch – usually the second one, which is larger. The parents sometimes destroy the first egg, but no one knows why they do this.

Erect-crested penguins have spiky crests. Unlike other crested penguins, they can raise and lower their crests. They are sociable birds, and make large rookeries, sometimes alongside Rockhoppers.

Like all crested penguins, Macaronis have short, red bills. They are the largest crested penguins, reaching about 60 centimetres in height. Royal penguins look similar, but they have white faces and throats.

▼ Male and female Macaroni penguins take turns to incubate their eggs.

Penguins in peril

Yellow-eyed penguins may become extinct during this century. They live in forests in New Zealand, but many trees have been cut down to build homes and farms. The penguins are attacked by predators that have been brought to the country, such as cats, dogs, foxes and ferrets. There are only about 1500 pairs of Yellow-eyed penguins left in the wild.

Some Adelie penguins have dangerous chemicals in their bodies. These have come from paints, pesticides and other substances that have been dumped in the sea. People have been treating the ocean like a rubbish tip, and the animals and plants that live there are now suffering because of the pollution.

◄ The habitats of the remaining Yellow-eyed penguins are now protected, but their numbers continue to fall.

Oil spills have caused the deaths of many penguins around the world. Huge ships (tankers) carry oil across the oceans. They often leak gallons of oil into the water, suffocating many marine animals. The oil damages the feathers of seabirds and many of them die.

The world is getting warmer, and this affects penguins. As the air is polluted the weather is changing. This is called global warming – and it will have an impact on habitats all over the world, especially the Antarctic, where the ice is starting to melt.

No one wants to see penguins disappear, but making the world a safer place for them is not an easy task. In the past, people have put the lives of penguins, and many other wild animals, in peril. People today will have to work hard to build a better future for all of the world's wildlife.

▲ The plumage of this African penguin has been covered in oil that leaked from a tanker. If the penguin tries to clean its feathers, it will be poisoned by the oil.

▼ Emperor penguins nest on winter ice. If this ice melts early, because of global warming (a change in the Earth's temperature), the species will struggle to survive.

Horses

Discover everything you need to know about horses
and ponies from the tiny Falabella to the giant Shire.

Hotbloods, warmbloods and coldbloods • Zebras
Anatomy • Colours and markings • Feeding • Habitats
Colts and fillies • Senses • The first horses
Asses, donkeys and mules • Wild ponies

Wild and wonderful

Strong, elegant and patient – horses have been loyal companions to humans for thousands of years. People have used horses to help them pull loads, plough fields and fight wars – without the help of horses, the story of human history would be very different. Today many people still rely on horses, ponies, donkeys and mules for transport. When they are free to gallop in a field, or live in the wild, we can truly appreciate the beauty and energy of these magnificent animals.

▶ All horses, wild or tame, enjoy the thrill of galloping at speed. They are sociable animals and prefer to live in groups, or herds.

Meet the family

Horses, ponies, zebras and asses all belong to the same animal family — the equids. All members of this family have a single toe on each foot and are called 'odd-toed' animals (unlike cows and deer, which have two toes on each foot). Like other animals with fur, horses are mammals and they give birth to live young, which they feed with milk.

▲ Zebras are easily recognized by their stripy coats. These wild equids live in Africa.

Equids live all over the world. Wild equids, such as zebras, live on grasslands where they can graze all day on plants. Horses that live and work with humans can be found almost everywhere across the world, and these are known as domestic horses.

Ponies are smaller than horses. Although horses and ponies are the same type of animal, they are different sizes. Horses are measured in 'hands', not centimetres, and a pony is a horse that is less than 14.2 hands (or 148 centimetres) tall. Ponies also have wider bodies and shorter legs than horses.

▶ A horse's height is measured from its feet to the top of its shoulders, which are known as 'withers' (see page 139).

Equids have manes of long hair on their heads and necks and thick, tufted tails. Their long legs, deep chests and powerful muscles allow them to run a long way at great speed without getting tired.

MEASURE IN HANDS

Normally we use centimetres and metres as units of measurement, but you can use anything you like – even your hands.

Measure the height of a table using your hands. Then ask an adult to measure it as well. Did you get the same measurement? If not, why not?

Wild horses live in large groups called herds. All horses, wild or domestic (tame), are very loyal to one another and can form close bonds with other animals, including humans. Since it is natural for horses to have company, domestic horses should always be kept together, or with other animals such as sheep and cows.

Horses are intelligent animals. They can communicate with each other by whinnying or braying, but, like many other animals, horses also sniff and smell one another to communicate. They also enjoy nuzzling and grooming each other's fur.

▼ In a herd, horses who get on well with each other will groom and nuzzle one another.

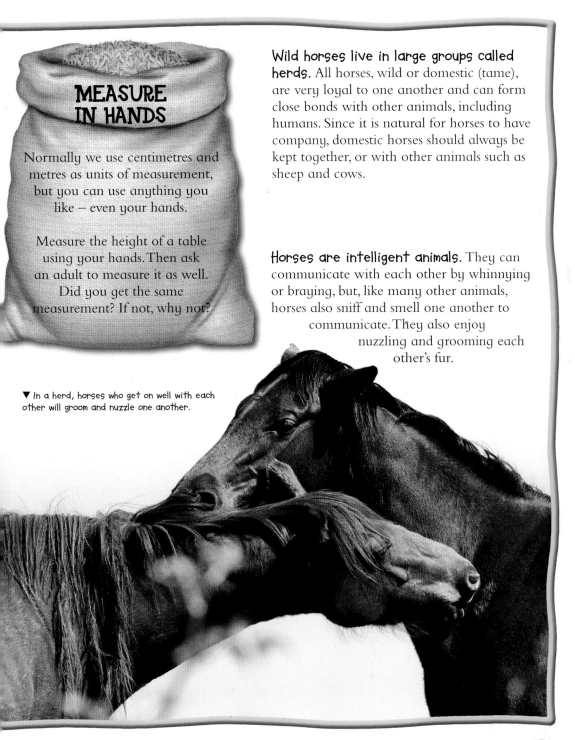

Inside out

▼ The features of a horse's skeleton, including extended leg bones and a rigid spine, allow it to run at speed for great distances.

Skull

Spine

Knee

Ribs

Femur

Fetlock

Horses have a bony framework called a skeleton. The skeleton supports their bodies and protects their organs. The skull protects the brain, and the ribs protect the lungs and heart. Bones are made from a hard material called calcium, but are full of tiny holes, which make them lightweight.

Croup

Dock

Domestic horses all belong to the same species, which means that they can mate with one another. Within the horse species there are lots of different types of horse, and these are called breeds. Breeds of horse differ in their appearance and in their personalities. A carthorse, for example, might have strong bones and a muscular body that is suited to pulling heavy loads, whereas a racehorse needs long legs and slender bones to run very fast.

Tail

Stifle

Thigh

Hock

Frog

Bars

Sole

Wall

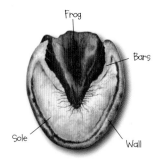

▲ A horseshoe is nailed to the 'wall' of a hoof.

Fetlock

All equids have hooves, which are made from keratin. Keratin is the same material that is found in fingernails, hair, fur and claws. Hoof edges can be trimmed without causing any pain to the horse. Domestic horses can be prone to having sore and damaged feet, because they often walk and run on hard, paved surfaces. It is important that their hooves are well looked after.

The parts of a horse's body that you can see are called 'the points of a horse'. Each point is given a special name and people who work with horses and ponies, or ride them, have to learn these names.

▼ Recognized terms or 'points' are used to pinpoint particular areas of a horse's body.

Poll
Crest
Ear
Withers
Back
Nostril
Muzzle
Shoulder
Breast
Forearm
Knee
Cannon bone
Fetlock
Hoof

▶ Metal horseshoes are heated and hammered into shape before fitting.

I DON'T BELIEVE IT!

It takes from nine months to one year for a horse to grow a completely new hoof. When a horse gallops, all of its weight is supported by just one slender hoof at a time.

A person who looks after hooves and makes horseshoes is called a farrier. The farrier cleans and trims the hoof, before attaching the iron shoe to the hoof by hammering long nails through the shoe and through the edge of the hoof wall. This doesn't hurt the horse at all.

Colours and markings

Star

Stripe

White face

Blaze

Snip

The fur of horses and ponies comes in a wide range of colours. The most common are bay (red-brown), chestnut (red-gold), grey (which can be almost white to dark grey), brown (dark bay) and black. There are also many other colour variations, such as dun (sandy brown), bright bay (light bay) and liver chestnut (dark chestnut).

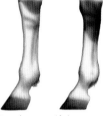

Over knee (stocking)　　Mid-cannon　　Fetlock

Half-pastern (sock)　　Crown　　Coronet

▲ White leg markings are described using the points of anatomy that the white hair covers.

Horses often have markings on their lower legs. These are called socks. White socks that extend above the knee are called stockings. Horses may have white marks elsewhere on their bodies – a white mark on the belly is called a 'flesh mark'.

White patches of fur on a horse's face are often used to help identify a horse. A 'stripe' is a narrow band of white that runs down the face, a 'blaze' is a broad band, a 'star' is a white mark on the forehead and a 'snip' is a patch of white between the horse's nostrils.

◀ A full description of a horse would include natural marks.

ODD ONE OUT!

Find the animal that has neither stripes nor spots:

1. Cheetah 2. Hover fly
3. Walrus 4. Coral snake
5. Song thrush

Answer: 3. Walrus

Some wild equids have stripes or dark marks along their spines. Zebras are the most famous of all striped animals, but other wild equids sometimes have stripy legs, or a stripe of black fur running from the mane to the tail. This darker stripe is called an 'eel stripe'.

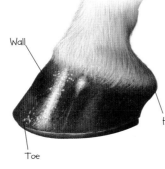

Wall

Heel

Toe

▲ A horse's hooves may be dark, light, plain or striped.

Horses' hooves can also be different colours. A horse with dark legs is likely to also have dark hooves. Pale horses, or those with white socks, often have hooves that are a pale colour – usually cream. Dark hooves are called 'blue' and pale hooves are called 'white'.

Some breeds of horse have large patches of different colours on their coats. These horses are called 'part-coloured'. Horses with patches of white and black fur are called 'piebald'. Horses with large patches of white and any other colour, apart from black, on their coats are called 'skewbald'.

▶ Horses that are referred to as 'piebald' usually have large, irregular patches of white and black hairs on their coat. Pinto horses are popular piebalds in the United States.

Hold your horses!

▼ Wild horses often run, or gallop, when they are scared. A stallion usually leads the way.

A horse's body is packed with muscles. These help it to run fast, jump and leap, and pull heavy loads. The world's fastest wild equid is the onager – an ass that can reach an incredible top speed of 78 kilometres an hour!

The way in which a horse moves is called the 'gait' or 'pace'. In the wild, horses move at their own pace and only have two gaits, walking slowly as they graze and galloping when they are frightened. Domestic horses are trained to perform at least four different gaits.

Walk

Trot

The 'walk' is the slowest gait. It has a four-beat rhythm. The horse places its left foreleg forwards, then its right hind (back) leg, followed by its right foreleg and then its left hind leg. The 'trot' is the next fastest gait and it has a two-beat rhythm. As the horse moves, two legs (for example, the left foreleg and the right hind leg) touch the ground at the same time, while the other two legs (the right foreleg and the left hind leg) are in the air.

The canter and gallop are the fastest two gaits. When a horse canters it has a three-beat rhythm, and there is a moment when all four of the horse's feet are off the ground. Galloping is the most exciting of the gaits. It is similar to the canter, but faster and with longer strides. Each foot strikes the ground separately. The moment when all four feet are in the air at the same time is called the suspension.

I DON'T BELIEVE IT!

At full gallop, Thoroughbred racehorses can reach speeds of over 60 kilometres an hour, even with riders on their backs.

▼ A rider can control their horse's gait. To change from one gait to another a rider presses their legs into the horse's body and pulls gently on the reins.

Canter

Gallop

Colts and fillies

Only a few hours after they are born, baby horses (foals) are able to stand up and walk around. Like the young of other hoofed animals, foals born in the wild are at risk of being hunted and caught by predators. For this reason, foals spend a long time – about 11 months – developing inside their mothers so they are ready to move and feed soon after they are born.

Mares – female horses – usually give birth to just one foal at a time. When a foal is born it rests for a few minutes, but soon attempts to stand and feed from its mother. The mare licks her newborn clean. She sniffs her foal to get used to its smell and the mother and foal whinny to one another, learning the sounds of each other's voices.

▶ In the first weeks of its life a foal stays next to its mother at all times. Mares can even sleep standing up, and are easily wakened if their youngster needs protection or reassurance.

Foals stay close to their mothers for the first two months of their lives. After this time the foals become braver and more adventurous, and will move away to investigate other members of the herd. Soon after this they begin to groom and play with other horses. When a young horse is between 12 and 24 months old, it is called a yearling. A female yearling is known as a filly, and a male yearling is known as a colt.

Up to 6 months

An expert can tell how old a horse is by looking at its teeth. The front, cutting, teeth are incisors and they are used to slice grass and other tender plants. As a horse ages, its incisors change from an oval shape to round, then become triangular and flattened. By examining the length and shape of a horse's teeth, it is possible to estimate its age.

At 5 years

At 15 years

At 25 years

WHAT TYPE OF ANIMAL AM I?

The young of animals are often given special names, like foal or calf. Use a dictionary to find out what type of animals these other youngsters are:

1. Eaglet 2. Gosling
3. Leveret 4. Maggot

Answers: 1. Eagle 2. Goose 3. Hare 4. Fly

▲ A horse's teeth change as it gets older. Teeth get gradually worn down with use and become more triangular in shape. Their surface markings also change.

Sensitive and smart

Horses have better senses of sight, hearing and smell than humans. Long ago the grasslands of the world were home to thousands of herds of equids, such as horses, zebra and asses. These grazing animals made good meals for predators. In order to keep themselves safe, horses needed to have highly developed senses of hearing, sight and smell so that they could detect any lurking predators.

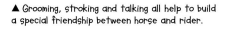
▲ Grooming, stroking and talking all help to build a special friendship between horse and rider.

Domestic horses and ponies like and need company. They can often become very close to the people who care for them, or ride them. Talking to horses may feel silly, but it isn't. They are such intelligent animals that they quickly begin to recognize voices, and can learn to understand simple words, such as 'no', 'stop' and 'go'.

I DON'T BELIEVE IT!

Horses have such good hearing that they have been known to sense earthquakes before humans are aware of them.

A horse's eye is twice as large as a human's eye, and is even bigger than an elephant's eye. Horses' eyes are positioned on the side of their heads, which means they can see in almost every direction. That's helpful when you always need to be on the look-out for a hungry predator.

Horses are able to recognize friends, both human and animal, by smell alone. Animals that live in groups have to be able to communicate with each other, and horses are no exception. Horses use the position of their ears to communicate their feelings – when their ears point backwards, horses are showing that they are scared or anxious.

A herd of wild horses includes only one adult male, called a stallion. There are normally only about seven horses in a herd – one stallion with his mares and foals. The stallion protects his family and fights any other males that come too close to the herd.

▼ Stallions start to fight when they are four to five years old. They will rear up and kick their rivals, and aim bites at the throat, neck, ears or tail.

147

Hungry as a horse!

Wild horses can spend between 16 and 20 hours a day feeding. The main bulk of their food is grass, which is difficult to digest. This means that horses need to eat a lot to get the energy that they need. Horses even eat during the night because they can see well in the dark and they only need a small amount of sleep. They will often nap for just a few minutes at a time, while still on their feet.

Horses are fussy eaters. They will spend time looking for a good patch of plants before they settle down to graze. Although they like grass, horses enjoy other plants-such as cocksfoot, wild white clover, dandelions and chicory. They use their flexible top lips to grab the plant, then bite off a clump with their incisor teeth.

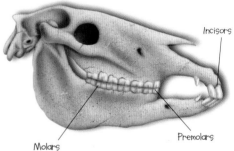

Incisors

Premolars

Molars

▶ Different types of teeth are used in eating. A horse's incisors cut and pull up plants. Its molars and premolars grind and mash the food. The surface of the teeth is worn down by about 3 millimetres every year.

Horses can't bring up food, so if they eat something poisonous it can kill them. Horses can poison themselves with the natural vegetation found in their fields, or in the trees and hedges surrounding their paddocks. Horses learn to avoid plants that taste bad, or cause them stomach pain, but not all dangerous plants have these obvious effects. Domestic horses and ponies should be kept in fields from which poisonous plants-such as foxglove, yew, bracken, buttercups, laurel and laburnum-have been removed.

Ragwort

◀ ▶ Ragwort, oak leaves and acorns are dangerous to horses. These plants should be removed from a horse's field.

Oak

Some domestic horses are given their food, so they do not have to graze all day. Their normal diet of grass and fresh plants is replaced with hay and other food. Horses have small stomachs, so they need to be given lots of small meals, rather than a few large ones. Hay is dry grass, so although horses enjoy it, they have to be given plenty of fresh water to help them digest it easily.

▼ Food — such as oats, barley, sugar beet and bran — are known as 'hard feed'. They may be mixed with chopped hay and straw and given to a horse or pony.

Removing a horse's or pony's droppings is called 'mucking out'. Horses produce lots of waste — manure — every day and clearing this away is an important job for anyone who owns a horse or pony. Manure is useful stuff — it can be left to rot, and then used in gardens or farms to put goodness back into the soil.

CHOOSE THE CORRECT WORD

1. Are animals that are active at night nocturnal or nautical?
2. Are rotting plants or manure called compost or comical?
3. Is tomahawk or toxin another name for poison?

Answers: 1. Nocturnal 2. Compost 3. Toxin

149

Habitats and homes

The first equids are thought to have lived in the area we now call America, when it was joined to other continents. A continent is a big region of land, such as Africa or North America, and long ago the continents were connected. From America, horses were able to spread to Europe, Asia and Africa.

After the last ice age, which ended about 10,000 years ago, millions of wild horses roamed the grasslands of Europe and Asia. They probably lived in herds, travelling great distances in search of food and water. The numbers of horses gradually decreased as the climate changed. Horses were also hunted by people, who used them for food and fur.

▼ Zebras now live in Africa but, like other equids, they originally came from North America.

Domestic horses are found all over the world. There are very few equids living in the wild now, but there are millions of domesticated horses that live or work with people who depend on them for transport or pulling loads.

▶ Most types of horses are domestic, but some wild horses still roam free.

The place where an animal lives is called its habitat. Wild horses are usually well-suited to their habitat. Those that live in cold areas may have very thick fur. The tarpan was an ancient type of horse with a coat that turned white during the snowy winter weather of its north European home.

Wild asses are found in western Asia and the Middle East. Asses are the ancestors of modern donkeys, which first lived in North Africa. Since then, donkeys have spread to other parts of the world, and are common in Europe.

▼ The ancestors of the Shire horse had to develop bulky bodies to help them survive the cold winters of northern Europe.

I DON'T BELIEVE IT!

About 10,000 years ago horses became extinct (died out) in the Americas. They were reintroduced by Spanish travellers about 500 years ago.

The first horses

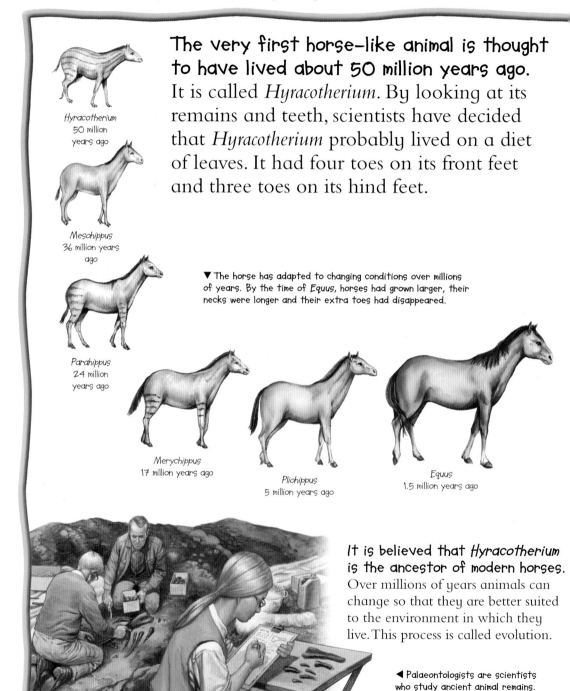

Hyracotherium
50 million
years ago

Mesohippus
36 million years
ago

Parahippus
24 million
years ago

The very first horse-like animal is thought to have lived about 50 million years ago. It is called *Hyracotherium*. By looking at its remains and teeth, scientists have decided that *Hyracotherium* probably lived on a diet of leaves. It had four toes on its front feet and three toes on its hind feet.

▼ The horse has adapted to changing conditions over millions of years. By the time of *Equus*, horses had grown larger, their necks were longer and their extra toes had disappeared.

Merychippus
17 million years ago

Pliohippus
5 million years ago

Equus
1.5 million years ago

It is believed that *Hyracotherium* is the ancestor of modern horses. Over millions of years animals can change so that they are better suited to the environment in which they live. This process is called evolution.

◄ Palaeontologists are scientists who study ancient animal remains.

MAKE A FAMILY TREE

You probably have some ancient relatives too! Look through old photograph albums and talk to your parents and grandparents to find out about members of your family. See how many years back you can trace. Do you look similar to any of your relatives?

There are only ten species of equids, but hundreds of different breeds of domestic horse. A species of animal includes any members of a group that can mate with one another to produce healthy young that are the same, or very similar. Breeds are different types, or varieties, of animals in one species.

Gradually, *Hyracotherium* evolved so that it could survive in a changing world. Thirty-six million years ago this ancient creature had disappeared, but a different horse-like animal lived – *Mesohippus*. It was the size of a sheep and had three toes on each foot, a long neck and a slender face.

▼ Unlike modern horses, who prefer to live on open grasslands and plains, *Hyracotherium* was a forest dweller.

Asses, donkeys and mules

An ass is a wild horse that is sure-footed and able to survive in very harsh conditions. Asses are shorter than most members of the horse family, and they are famous for their ability to live in places where there is little food or water. Wild asses are found mainly in Africa and Asia, where rain rarely falls and the ground is stony. Asses can survive on a diet of dry grass and thorny shrubs and bushes.

Long before farmers had tractors, they used animals to work in their fields. Onagers, which are a type of ass, were probably the first animals that were used to pull ploughs and carts. They are extremely fast runners, strong and reliable. Today, these gentle creatures are in danger of extinction.

Przewalski's wild horse looks similar to an ass, with its short stocky body. The last free Przewalski's horse was seen in the 1970s, in Mongolia. Today, these unusual beasts are mostly kept in zoos or parks, but a small herd has now been put back into the wild.

◄ Przewalski's horse is heavily built. It has a large head, thick neck and short legs.

▶ Donkeys and mules have often been used to carry heavy loads. This mule train, under attack, is carrying treasure.

Donkeys are asses that have been domesticated. They are used to carry people or goods, and for farming. They are very strong and can live in harsh habitats, often walking for many miles in the heat with little food or water.

▼ Donkeys are popular with tourists at the seaside, where they carry children down the beach.

MATING GAME

When two different species of animals are mated, their youngster (like a mule) is called a 'hybrid'. Can you guess the parents of these hybrids?

1. Geep 2. Tigon
3. Wholphin

Answers: 1. Goat and sheep
2. Tiger and lion 3. Whale and dolphin

If a female horse mates with a male donkey, the foal is called a mule. Mules combine the horse's strength with the donkey's ability to keep working in difficult conditions. If a male horse mates with a female donkey, the foal is called a hinny. Mules and hinnies are sterile, which means that they cannot have any foals themselves.

On the African plains

Zebras are wild horses that have startling patterns of black-and-white striped fur. They are found in Africa, where they live on the huge grasslands known as the savannah, along with other grazing or browsing creatures such as giraffes, wildebeests and antelopes.

There are three types, or species, of zebra – Grevy's, mountain and Burchell's. A Grevy's zebra lives further north than the other two species. It is the tallest of the three types and has very thin stripes, particularly on its face. The mountain zebra has a dark muzzle and thick black stripes on its rump. It is in danger of becoming extinct. The most common of the three types is Burchell's zebra.

Grevy's zebra

Burchell's zebra

Mountain zebra

▲ Zebra types can be identified by the pattern of stripes on their fur.

▼ The common, or Burchell's, zebra has broad horizontal stripes that extend under the belly.

No one knows for sure why zebras have stripes. It was thought that the patterns might confuse predators. Or it may be for purposes of identification – each zebra has a unique pattern of stripes, and a zebra can recognize another member of its herd just by its pattern of stripes.

There was a fourth type of zebra – the quagga – but it is now extinct. Quaggas lived in southern Africa, in herds of up to a hundred individuals. Like other zebras, they lived on grasslands and spent most of their day grazing. They were ruthlessly hunted by European settlers and the last one died in 1883.

Horses and ponies in the past

No one knows for sure when horses and ponies were first used by people for riding, pulling or carrying things. However, there are pictures of men on horseback that are more than 4000 years old! Since ancient times, horses, ponies, asses and donkeys have helped humans explore their world.

▼ This horse–drawn machine, called a 'seed drill', dropped seeds into a ploughed field and helped make farming more efficient.

For thousands of years, horses went to war. In ancient Persia (now Iran) and Rome, horses pulled chariots that took soldiers wielding swords and spears into battle, or to entertain crowds in large arenas.

◄ In the Middle Ages, kings and knights led their armies to war on horses chosen for their strength and obedience.

Horses have been used in farming and for carrying or pulling heavy weights. The strongest members of the horse family have been chosen by farmers to help them move carts weighed down with crops, or to plough fields and carry water. In most modern countries, machinery has replaced horses, but across the world many people still rely on their horses to help them grow their crops.

The United States of America was explored by settlers with horses. The USA covers a vast area. Without horses and mules it would have been very difficult for European travellers to make their way across the huge continent. Hundreds of horse-drawn wagons formed a winding trail as they travelled west to set up new towns and farming communities.

▶ Annie Oakley was an American rodeo star and sharp shooter.

A thousand years ago, medieval soldiers took part in tournaments on horseback. They sat astride their large and powerful horses, which had to carry their riders and heavy metal armour too, as they jousted with one another to prove their courage and strength.

EXPLORE!

Discover more about an area near you and arrange a trip there with family or friends.
You will need:
map food drinks
Choose a place you have never visited before, so like a real explorer, you'll see everything for the first time. Decide how you will travel there, and plan carefully. Make sure you take an adult with you when you go.

Wild ponies

Ponies are usually smaller than horses, with wider bodies and shorter legs. They often come from areas of the world where they have had to struggle to survive, so they show great stamina. Ponies are usually sure-footed, which means that they can easily get about on steep hillsides and rocky plains. Wild ponies have often lost their habitats to humans, but some breeds still live on the moors and grasslands of the world.

▲ The Highland is the largest of the Scottish breeds and can survive where food is scarce.

Connemara ponies originally came from Ireland, but they are now bred throughout Europe. Connemaras have been bred with Arab and Thoroughbred horses, and they have inherited speed and good jumping ability from these famous horse breeds. Connemaras are strong, sturdy and intelligent. They make good competition horses and are popular with both adults and children.

▶ Wild Connemara ponies have lived on the moors of western Ireland since the 16th century.

TRUE OR FALSE?

1. Ponies can suffer from sunburn.
2. Some horses are allergic to dust.
3. Little bugs, called mites, can live in ponies' ears, making them itchy.

Answers: All are true

Tiny Shetland ponies first arrived in Scotland about 10,000 years ago, from Scandinavia. They live in harsh conditions, which has led to the breed developing great strength. Shetland ponies are measured in inches, not hands, and they stand up to 40 inches (102 centimetres) tall. For their size, Shetlands are probably the strongest of all horse and pony breeds.

▼ Shetland ponies have thick fur and manes to protect them from the cold. They have large noses and nostrils so they can warm the air before it reaches their lungs.

New Forest ponies have been living wild for about a thousand years. They live in protected woodlands and heaths of Hampshire in southern England. The ponies can graze and mate freely. This type of pony can also be tamed and used in riding stables, where it is particularly popular with children.

Two of the most famous breeds of wild pony are the Dartmoor and Exmoor. These sturdy ponies can survive the difficult conditions found on the moors — they have to be tough enough to cope with rain, snow, biting winds and the poor grazing. The Exmoor is one of the oldest breeds in the world, and dates back as far as the last ice age — 10,000 years ago! Tame Dartmoor ponies are often used for riding lessons, as they are strong and they jump well.

Ponies as pets

In the past, ponies were used to haul carts and work on farms, but today they are most often kept as pets. Children who want to learn how to ride usually have their first lessons on a pony. Ponies are good-natured animals. They are reliable and patient, so boys and girls can often form very close friendships with them.

Fell ponies are famous for their ability to work very hard. They were once used in mines and on farms, and could travel hundreds of kilometres in one week, pulling carts. Fell ponies are only 14 hands (142 centimetres) high, but they are strong enough to carry adults and they are popular ponies for children.

◀ Fell ponies are usually black or dark brown, occasionally with small white markings. Their bodies are deep, their legs are short and strong and they have long, thick tails.

▲ Falabella horses are so small they can even be dwarfed by a dog! Falabellas have large heads, slender legs and thick manes and tails.

The little Falabella is the smallest of all the horse breeds. It is a very new type of horse, which has been created by the Falabella family of Argentina, who mated Shetland ponies with Thoroughbred horses. A Falabella only stands about 7 hands (71 centimetres) tall, but it is often called a miniature horse rather than a pony because of its horse-like character and body shape. Falabellas are too small to be ridden, but they are popular as pets. Falabella foals are usually only 4 hands (41 centimetres) tall.

Welsh mountain ponies make excellent riding ponies. They are divided into four different types – Section A, B, C and D. Welsh Section A ponies come from the Welsh mountains. Section B, C and D ponies have been developed by breeding Section A ponies with other types of horse or pony. They are often used for jumping or driving.

▶ Welsh cobs make good driving ponies – this means they can be used for pulling a cart or trap.

Hotblood horses

Horse breeds are divided into three main groups, called hotbloods, warmbloods and coldbloods. Hotbloods are ancient and very pure breeds that originally came from North Africa and the Middle East. They are very elegant and fast runners. Coldbloods come from northern Europe and they are large, heavy, strong horses. Warmbloods were developed by mating hotbloods with coldbloods.

Although horses come in all sorts of shapes and sizes, they are divided into breeds. Within each breed, the horses are similar in personality and appearance. By mating a horse from one breed with a horse of another breed, people (called breeders) have been able to create new and different types of horse, such as warmbloods.

The most famous of all hotbloods is the Arab. These lively and speedy horses first lived in the desert regions of the Middle East. They are said to be the oldest domestic horse breed in the world, as well as the most beautiful. Arabs are small, but they are famous for their stamina. Like Thoroughbreds and Akhal-Tekés, Arabs are a high-spirited breed and are not usually considered suitable horses for young or inexperienced riders.

▼ Although Arabs are not as fast as Thoroughbreds, they gallop with a wonderful, flowing movement and they can run for a long time before getting tired.

Thoroughbreds are the world's fastest domestic horses. These hotbloods were first bred in England about 400 years ago, to create fast horses for competitions. They are still used as racehorses, or to breed with other types of horse and pony. Thoroughbreds are both strong and quick, and for these reasons they are thought of as one of the best horses to ride, but they can have difficult personalities and are hard to handle.

The Akhal-Teké is a hotblood horse that has been bred in the Middle East for thousands of years. These brave and tough horses are unusual looking, with long and slender bodies that are coated in a thin layer of golden fur. Akhal-Tekés are the world's greatest long-distance runners, and can even cope with the extreme heat and dryness of the desert.

I DON'T BELIEVE IT!

Akhal-Teké hotbloods have been known to travel over 4000 kilometres in just 84 days, surviving on only a tiny amount of food and water.

Warmblood horses

Most horse breeds of the world are warmbloods. Despite their name, the blood of warmbloods is exactly the same temperature as that of hotbloods and coldbloods! The name refers to where different types of horses come from. Hotbloods first came from desert areas, while coldbloods came from cold countries of the north – and warmbloods are a mixture of both!

▼ A Lipizzaner stallion performs a movement called the 'levade'.

▼ Quarter horses have become famous for being those ridden by cowboys when they tend their cattle. They were bred for riding and farm work.

The Quarter horse is said to be the most popular horse in the world. It works hard, but it also has a calm and patient personality. Quarter horses were first bred in the USA, about 350 years ago. They combine great strength with agility – they can stop, start and change direction very quickly.

The Spanish Riding School of Vienna is known throughout the world for the athletic tricks performed by its Lipizzaner horses. These grey warmbloods have Spanish ancestors (which is how the Riding School got its name) and they are trained to perform special movements, such as jumps and kicks. The movements are said to be based on medieval tricks of war that were used to evade enemy soldiers. It takes many years to train just one horse.

Camargue horses have been called the 'wild white horses of the sea'. These beautiful white warmbloods come from the bleak and windswept Rhône region of southern France. As a result, they are extremely tough. It is thought that they are related to the primitive horses that appear in French cave drawings, which are about 17,000 years old. There are herds of wild Camargue horses, but domesticated ones are used by local cowboys to round up wild black bulls.

MAKE TASTY HORSESHOES

You will need:
packet of bread mix

1. Follow the instructions carefully to mix the dough and knead it.
2. Make small balls that you can then mould into strips and shape into horseshoes.
3. Leave the dough to rise, then sprinkle with sesame seeds and bake in the oven. Eat the horseshoes with butter and jam while they are still warm.

One of the most unusual-looking warmbloods is the Appaloosa. It is known for its strikingly patterned coat, which can be a variety of different colours. This American breed got its name from the Palouse River in the USA. It was bred during the 18th century by a Native American tribe, who wanted to create strong and agile working horses.

▶ There are five Appaloosa coat patterns: marble, blanket, leopard, snowflake and frost. Shown here are blanket (white quarters and loins, sometimes with dark spots) and frost (dark background with white speckles).

Coldblood horses

Coldblood horses come from the cooler regions of the world, and they are the largest and strongest of all horse types. Coldbloods have been bred for their immense power, and they have been used to pull heavy loads for hundreds of years, particularly on farms. They have wide backs, muscle-packed bodies and thick, short legs. They usually have very calm, docile natures.

▼ Heavy horses carried medieval knights into war. They are the ancestors of breeds — such as the Shire horse (in Britain) and the Percheron (in France).

Coldbloods are also known as 'heavy' or 'draught' horses. Before trains and motor vehicles were invented, these horses worked hard as they ploughed fields, pulled boats along canals or hauled carts. In medieval times, these heavyweights were needed to help carry knights to fields of war.

Heavy horses are often dressed up and shown in competitions. The owners of these magnificent creatures often travel to country shows and fairs where they give demonstrations to show their horses' strength and power. The horses' manes are braided and plaited, and they are decorated with brasses and gleaming harnesses.

The Shire is often called the greatest of all draught horses. It is tall, strong and very gentle. It gets its name from the English counties of Derbyshire, Lincolnshire, Staffordshire and Leicestershire, where it was first bred. Shire horses carried English Medieval knights into battle, and also worked on farms and in cities.

I DON'T BELIEVE IT!

Horses rarely live to be older than 30 years, but an English draught horse, called Old Billy, is said to have made it to the grand age of 62!

▲ Shire horses can stand more than 18 hands (180 centimetres) tall and are probably the largest heavy horses. They are usually black, bay, brown or grey in colour, and their legs often have long white stockings. Most heavy horses have wispy fur, called feathers, around their hooves.

Suffolk Punches are coldbloods that are all related to a single male horse, which was born in 1768. Suffolks were bred to work on farms but their distinctive chestnut colour makes them a popular breed at shows and competitions.

Monkeys and Apes

Read all about our closest animal relatives
and discover how and where they live.

Tamarins • Communication • Spider monkeys
Baboons • Macaques • Intelligence • Family life
Gibbons • Bonobos • Chimps • Orang-utans
Gorillas • Conservation

Our closest cousins

Monkeys and apes are fascinating creatures. They are our closest relatives and belong to a family of animals called primates. These animals can range in size from the tiny mouse lemur, which is no bigger than your hand, to the giant silverback gorilla. They may not all look alike, but primates share an important characteristic – they are very intelligent creatures.

▶ These douc langur monkeys belong to the same family of animals as humans – primates.

What is a primate

Primates such as monkeys and apes are covered in fur or hair and the young feed on their mothers' milk. They have big brains and can work out solutions to difficult problems. Primates have been known to learn new skills and teach them to their young.

Primates are mammals. This means that they have back bones and warm-blooded bodies. They are divided into three groups – prosimians, such as bushbabies, monkeys, such as baboons, and apes, such as gorillas.

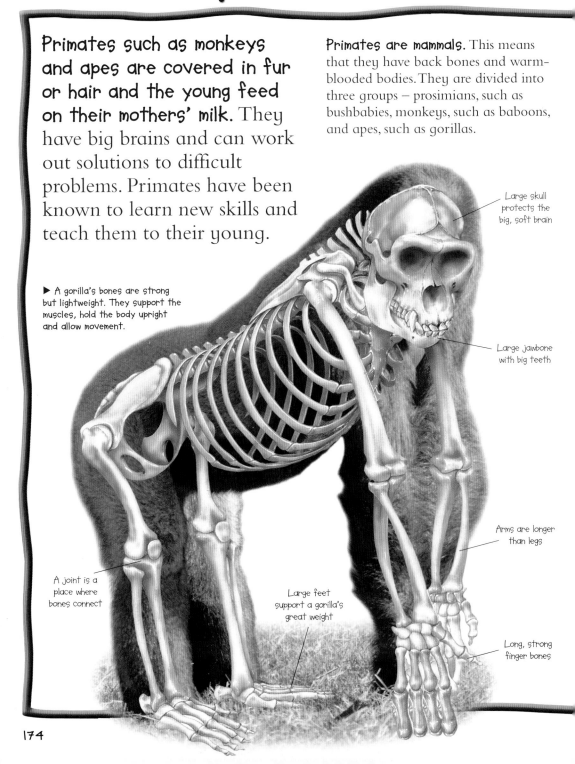

▶ A gorilla's bones are strong but lightweight. They support the muscles, hold the body upright and allow movement.

Large skull protects the big, soft brain

Large jawbone with big teeth

Arms are longer than legs

A joint is a place where bones connect

Large feet support a gorilla's great weight

Long, strong finger bones

Unlike many other animals, primates have large eyes at the front of their heads. This allows them to focus clearly on objects in front of them. Since most primates live in trees and leap between branches, this is a very useful feature. Unlike most other creatures, primates can see in colour.

▼ Primates' hands and feet can grab, hold, pinch and probe. Most primates can grip objects and tools precisely in their hands.

Tarsier hand

Tarsier foot

Spider monkey hand

Spider monkey foot

Chimpanzee hand   Chimpanzee foot

Primates have hands that are very similar to ours. Instead of paws and claws, they have fingers and flat fingernails. They can bring their forefingers and thumbs together in a delicate pinching movement.

Primates prefer to live in groups. They often live with their families, or large groups of related families. Primates communicate with one another in lots of ways – using sound, scent, touch and movement. Young primates usually stay with their families for years while they learn how to survive.

▶ In many primate groups, such as the baboons shown here, adults help the mother by finding food and helping to look after the baby. Males will also gather food and play with the young.

Bushbabies

Bushbabies are beautiful, bright-eyed animals that are active at night and sleep in the day. They belong to the group of primates called prosimians, and live in Africa. Here, they make their homes in tall forest trees. Bushbabies need their large eyes to see well in the dark, and their sensitive ears listen for the sound of insects and other prey at night.

▲ The slow loris moves slowly to avoid attracting the attention of predators. It moves carefully towards its prey and then lunges.

▼ Lesser bushbabies are only about 15 centimetres in length, but they can make giant leaps of up to 10 metres.

1. As a lesser bushbaby leaps up, it holds its body straight

2. The body curls up in the air, with legs tucked in tight

3. In just one jump, the bushbaby can cover 10 metres

Bushbabies are quick movers and can even catch scorpions and spiders by surprise. They use their nimble little fingers to grasp hold of their prey, such as crickets or lizards, and gobble up every last piece.

▶ Eyesight is very important to a tarsier and each eye is heavier than its brain. Tarsiers also have large ears that pick up the quietest of sounds.

Lorises live in the forests of Southeast Asia. Like bushbabies, they are closely related to monkeys and apes and lead similar lives. These furry animals spend most of their time in trees, where they move carefully and slowly through the leaves, searching for food. During the day they curl up in their hiding places and sleep.

Tarsiers are odd-looking primates. Their eyes are so big, they actually take up half the space in their heads! These primates can swivel their heads almost the whole way round, so they can watch what's going on behind them and look out for predators, or other animals to eat. They live in Southeast Asia and at night they leap with great ease through the trees.

4. Unlike most jumping animals, the bushbaby lands with its hind feet first

I DON'T BELIEVE IT!

Bushbabies have two tongues! When eating gum – a sticky substance made by trees – they use their teeth to scrape it off the bark. Then they wipe the gum off their teeth with their second tongue!

177

Leaping lemurs

Lemurs are long-legged primates that live in just one place on Earth – Madagascar. This large island in the Indian Ocean is home to lots of animals that aren't found anywhere else. Many of them, including lemurs, are dying out – partly because their forest homes are being cut down.

Ring-tailed lemurs are elegant, curious creatures. Unlike most other lemurs, they spend a lot of time on the ground and as they walk they hold their boldly-patterned tails high in the air. These primates rub their tails with smelly substances from under their arms. When two rival lemurs meet they wave their stinky tails at one another!

▼ As well as being agile tree climbers, ring-tailed lemurs can move swiftly on the ground.

QUIZ
Most lemurs live in trees. What word is used to describe the place where an animal lives?

1. Halibut 2. Habit
3. Habitat

Answer:
3. Habitat

178

▼ An aye-aye uses its long middle finger to probe into cracks in a tree and pick out tasty grubs to eat.

Newborn lemurs are soon strong enough to grasp onto their mothers' fur. As a female travels around between trees, her infant holds on tight, safe from predators. However the youngster is always at risk of falling to its death should it let go for a second.

The aye-aye is probably the ugliest primate. This shaggy-haired lemur builds its nest in the forks of trees and emerges at night to eat insects and fruit. Using its large ears, the aye-aye can hear beetles as they scratch around on the forest floor. An aye-aye's middle finger is unusually long – ideal for digging into wood and pulling out grubs to eat.

▶ Sifakas can stand upright and run on their hind feet. They can leap 10 metres between branches.

Indris and sifakas are types of large lemur that are very close to extinction. They are gentle, plant-eating animals with loud voices, and can be heard calling from several kilometres away. Farmers and loggers are cutting down the forests where they live, and they are also hunted for meat.

Bright and bold

The beautiful golden lion tamarin is a familiar sight in zoos and wildlife parks. These brightly coloured monkeys live in the tropical forests of Central and South America, but many of them are kept in captivity. At least 500 golden lion tamarins that were born in zoos have been released into the wild.

Tamarins belong to the group of primates called monkeys. All monkeys have tails, even if it's only a little stump. They are more intelligent than prosimians, but less intelligent than apes. Monkeys are divided into two groups – New World monkeys from the Americas and Old World monkeys from Europe, Asia and Africa.

The black-headed lion tamarin lives in just three places in Brazil. It is one of the world's rarest monkeys and it's thought there are no more than 250 of them left alive, and even those few are fighting for survival. The reason for this is that their forest homes are being cut down so that wood from the trees can be sold.

◀ Golden lion tamarins live in family groups of three to seven monkeys that stay together in one area, or territory. They fight with other groups that come into their territory.

It's not just mums who look after babies — dads do too. In most animal families, it's the mother that cares for the youngsters, but in tamarin families, the fathers share this important job. The mothers may feed the babies, but it's the fathers who carry the young on their backs, protecting them from owls, hawks, wild cats and snakes.

I DON'T BELIEVE IT!

Not many monkeys have moustaches — but little emperor tamarins do! Other tamarins have crowns of white hair, beards or tufts of fur on their ears.

Communication

Monkeys and apes may not use words to communicate, but they are good at letting each other know how they are feeling. Like humans, they can move their faces and make different noises to show their emotions.

CHIMP FACES

Do you look like a chimp? Stand in front of a mirror and copy the chimp faces shown on this page. Then make your own, 'happy', 'worried' and 'pay me attention' faces. Is it easy to copy a chimp? Are your human expressions anything like the chimp's?

Play face

◀ The chimp's eyes are relaxed and its mouth is open, but the top teeth are covered by the lip. Happy chimps can even make laughing noises.

Worried face

▲ The lips are pulled right back and all the teeth are on show. The chimp makes high screeching sounds.

Leaving a strong smell behind you is a good way to let other animals know you've been around! Lots of creatures, not just monkeys and apes, leave their smell on trees and the ground to warn other animals to stay away. Monkey smells are made in special body parts called glands, which are often around the animals' rumps (bottoms).

Colours can be used to communicate. A healthy male mandrill baboon has a brightly coloured face and rump. This probably helps a female pick the best male with which to mate.

◀ If a young chimp is being ignored by its mother, it pushes its lips out and whimpers or makes a short hooting sound until she notices it.

Pouting face

Apes can use beating sounds to show they are angry. Large male gorillas, for example, slap their cupped hands loudly against their chests. They also beat the ground with their fists, making noises that scare off other males or enemies.

Howler monkeys are the loudest of all primates. When they get together in a group, or troop, and start calling, the noise can be heard up to 3 kilometres away! They use this type of communication to tell other howler monkeys to keep their distance.

▼ Apes and monkeys use noises such as screeches and grumbles to communicate. The loud calls of these howler monkeys, which are more like roars, can echo through the forest and warn others to keep out of their territory.

On the move

It's easy to fall when you are leaping between tall trees – and that's why many monkeys have tails that can grip branches. Some monkeys' tails work like an extra arm or leg, and can be moved and controlled in the same way we can move our four limbs.

New World monkeys are very similar to Old World monkeys, but they spend almost all of their lives in jungles or rainforests. Their tails are particularly useful for grabbing hold of branches and are called prehensile tails.

When monkeys dart around the treetops they can find plenty of food. There are fruits, nuts, seeds, insects, lizards and birds' eggs to be found in the upper layers of a rainforest.

▲ The tail of a woolly spider monkey has bald patches that allow for a better grip.

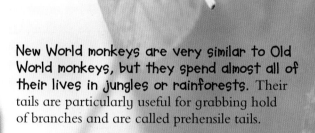

Squirrel monkeys often live in large groups with more than 50 members, but some groups may number as many as 200! These little primates have tails that are longer than their bodies and they are extremely agile and acrobatic in the treetops.

Squirrel monkeys are so light and nimble they can run along branches that are no more than 2 centimetres thick. They spend almost all their lives in trees and rarely come to the ground. When they do, they scurry around looking for food, or spend a little while playing.

◀ This squirrel monkey has wrapped its tail around a tree for extra support.

WHERE IN THE WORLD?

New World monkeys come from South and Central America. Use an atlas to find which of these countries are in the Americas:

Bolivia Brazil Ghana Peru
India Sri Lanka Panama

Answer:
Bolivia Brazil Peru Panama

▲ Capuchin monkeys scamper through the treetops, foraging for food. They eat a wide variety of fruits. They also catch insects and other small animals.

Spider monkeys

If you are a monkey, it's a good idea to spend most of your time up in the trees. Hidden amongst the leaves and branches, it's easier to stay out of the reach of other animals that may want to eat you. Although big cats such as jaguars can climb trees, they can't chase monkeys onto the thinnest branches.

Spider monkeys are some of the fastest, most nimble of the primate climbers. Their arms, legs and tails are extremely long, and they can hang from a tree by a single limb or tail. They usually run along a tree's branches with their tails curled over their backs, and it's rare for them to walk around on the ground.

Spider monkeys can travel up to 5 kilometres a day browsing for their favourite food of ripe fruit. During the dry season, from July to September, there is less food around, so the monkeys spend most of their day resting and saving energy.

THAT'S HANDY!

Find out just how useful your hands are!
You will need:
a big bowl of cold water   apples
Put the apples in the bowl and place it
on the floor. Keep your hands behind
your back and grab an apple out of
the bowl, using just your mouth.
It's not easy.

◀ High up in the forest canopy,
black-handed spider monkeys hang
by a hand, foot or tail and swing
at speed between branches.

Spider monkeys are noisy animals and
make loud barking calls if they're
scared. This warns the rest of the troop
to beware, because a predator, such as a
wild cat or snake, may be around. If some
members of the family are separated,
they make whinnying noises until they
find one another.

While many primates use their
thumbs to grip, some spider monkeys
don't even have any! Despite being
thumbless, these agile animals can hold
onto branches by using a hand and four
long fingers like a hook.

Baboons

Not all monkeys live in trees – some prefer to spend most of their time on the ground. Baboons, for example, are Old World monkeys that usually only climb trees to sleep. In fact, most baboons live in dry, rocky or grassy places where there are few trees. Some baboons even sleep on cliff faces.

Baboons may not be great climbers, but they are excellent swimmers. Those that live by the sea often wade into the water to find crabs and other shelled creatures to eat.

▶ Baboons come to waterholes and rivers to drink. They are vulnerable to attack and keep a lookout for predators between sips.

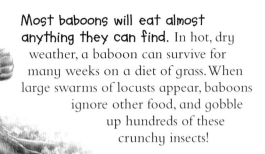

▶ A baboon rummages through elephant dung, finding seeds and insects to eat.

Most baboons will eat almost anything they can find. In hot, dry weather, a baboon can survive for many weeks on a diet of grass. When large swarms of locusts appear, baboons ignore other food, and gobble up hundreds of these crunchy insects!

The largest baboons of all are called chacma baboons and they live in southern Africa. Male chacmas are much bigger than the females, and can grow to nearly one metre in length. Their tails are the same length as their bodies, which are strong and stout. Baboons walk on all four legs, and hold their tails over their backs as they walk or run.

▼ Baboons, such as this gelada, bear their teeth as a sign of aggression. However geladas are actually less aggressive than other baboons. They are also the only monkeys that eat mostly grass.

Baboons hunt other animals. With their powerful limbs, large teeth and quick intelligence, these animals make fearsome predators. They can run at speed, and have been known to catch other mammals, such as gazelles. Males often fight one another at mating time, and the strongest males become leaders of the group.

Macaques

There is one group of monkeys that has been able to make its home in all sorts of places – the macaques. There are 15 different types of macaque and they live in North Africa and Asia in forests and swamps. In these places it can be snowy, or hot and dry.

▲ Rhesus monkeys can find food in towns, and are sometimes considered pests. This monkey is living in a temple in Thailand.

In the Indian state of Uttar Pradesh there are groups of macaques called rhesus monkeys. They find shelter in buildings or beneath cars in cities and towns. Like most macaques they are able to eat whatever food they come across, such as fruit, berries, insects, seeds and flowers.

Crab-eating macaques live in Asian forests where the weather is always hot and rainy. At night they huddle together on branches that hang over rivers. If they get scared, they simply drop into the water and swim away!

◄ Crab-eating macaques hunt for crabs, shrimps, frogs and octopuses to eat in mangrove swamps.

Like most other primates, macaques eat soil. No one knows for sure why they do this but there are probably two reasons. Firstly, soil contains important minerals, such as iron, calcium and sodium that are good for the monkeys' health. The second reason is that some soils appear to contain substances that kill small worms living inside the monkeys' bodies.

The fluffy pale fur and pink face of a Japanese macaque is a startling sight. These monkeys don't just look peculiar – they behave rather strangely too! Japanese macaques live in the cold mountains of Honshu, in Japan, but one troop has found a great way to keep warm – they bathe in the hot-water springs that bubble up from the ground!

▼ Bathing in hot-water springs is a regular winter pastime for Japanese macaques. Having hot baths is one way to survive the extreme cold.

Fascinating faces

Many monkeys and apes look so like humans that we find their faces fascinating. Some primates, though, are simply odd-looking!

Black-and-white colobus monkeys live in Africa where they've been hunted for their amazing coats for hundreds of years. When these monkeys leap between trees, they use their long, fluffy tails to steer or change direction.

The proboscis monkey is a very peculiar primate. 'Proboscis' means 'nose' and it's easy to see how this animal got its name. Although the baby monkeys are born with normal-sized noses, they soon start to grow, and by the time they are adult males, proboscis monkeys have long, droopy snouts.

Male proboscis monkey

Female proboscis monkey

◀ The male proboscis monkey has a bigger nose than the female. It can be up to 8 centimetres in length. The male honks loudly to mark his territory and to frighten predators.

Baby proboscis monkey

▶ Red uakaris are shy and unaggressive monkeys, despite their fierce red faces.

Gelada baboons may not be pretty, but they are difficult to ignore! They have long, expressive faces and bare chests, which have bright red or pink triangular patches. These monkeys have thick brown fur on their bodies, which grows long around the shoulders, head and neck on males.

The red uakari monkey looks as if he's lost all the fur from his face, but he's meant to look this ugly! Young red uakaris are born with normal amounts of hair on their pale pink faces, but by the time they are about two years old, their faces have become bald and red.

De Brazza's monkeys look smart and tidy, with their neat white beards, dark eyebrows and orange crowns. These African monkeys live on a diet of fruit, flowers, seeds, leaves and lizards. They call to one another with loud, booming sounds across the dense rainforests where they live.

◀ De Brazza's monkeys mark their territory but they avoid intruders rather than challenge them.

193

Intelligent creatures

Monkeys are clever, and apes are even smarter. All primates have big brains, and they put them to good use. When faced with a problem, the most intelligent monkeys and apes may be able to work out a solution and some of them even use tools, such as sticks and stones. Chimpanzees are probably the most intelligent apes of all.

Many monkeys and apes use tools to help them get food. Capuchin monkeys smash tough fruits with sticks of wood until they can break into them. Youngsters often copy the adults, but they aren't usually strong enough to succeed!

▲ Capuchin monkeys use a variety of techniques to break open nuts. This capuchin is using a rock to crack palm nuts.

HOW CLEVER ARE YOU?

Can you learn a new skill?

Choose from one of these three activities and ask a grown-up to teach you how to do it:

1. Make a sandwich
2. Plant a seed and help it grow
3. Learn how to whistle

Monkeys and apes are quick to learn new things. Youngsters watch their parents and older members of the family, and copy them when they collect food or use tools. This ability to learn has been put to good use by people in Southeast Asia, who have taught pig-tailed macaques to climb palm trees and throw down coconuts for them!

◀ Pig-tailed macaques have been trained to climb trees and collect coconuts. They scramble up the trees, twist the coconuts from the top and drop them to the ground.

Orang-utans find many ways to use leaves, and have been seen using them as fly-swats, 'toilet paper' and umbrellas! These apes are so clever they can collect stacks of sticks to hold prickly fruit while they break it open. They can connect short sticks together to make one long one, make swings from rope and they have even been seen stacking boxes on top of one another to create a ladder.

Baboons that live in Saudi Arabia filter their own drinking water! These clever primates dig holes in the ground next to ponds. They watch the water filter through the sandy soil before drinking it. The sand stops dirt and bugs from passing through and this means the baboons are less likely to become ill.

▶ Orang-utans sometimes hold leafy branches over their heads to shelter from the rain and the sun.

Family life

Most monkeys and apes live in families and eat, sleep and play together. Primates are described as social animals. This means they prefer to stay together as groups – and they can be sociable because they are so good at communicating with one another. A group may have just two members, or several hundred.

New families begin with mating. This is when the males and females get together to start families. Male monkeys and apes often have to impress the females to persuade them to mate, and they sometimes do this by fighting off other males. It's usually the strongest and biggest males who get the most mates.

▶ Young baboons start to explore away from their mothers when they are two or three months old.

The time it takes for a baby to grow inside its mother's body is called a pregnancy. Female monkeys and apes are pregnant for around five to nine months – animals with longer pregnancies tend to be more intelligent, but give birth to young that are quite helpless. Just like human babies, monkey infants rely on their mothers for everything.

◄ This baby silvered langur monkey depends on its mother for everything. Its bright orange coat will last until the infant is about three months old.

Young primates spend a lot of time with adults, watching and learning. Youngsters watch their mothers eating plants, and learn which ones are good to eat, and which ones may be harmful. They also enjoy playing – but if a young gorilla jumps on its dad one too many times, it may get a gentle push to warn it to stop!

Silvered langurs have silver-grey fur, but their babies are born bright orange. After three months their striking colour fades as grey hair grows. No one knows why the youngsters look so different, but it may remind older langurs to treat them more gently.

197

Gibbons

1. Preparing to move, a lar gibbon swings its body forward, gripping the branch with both hands.

2. One hand lets go of the branch behind as the gibbon moves forward.

Gibbons are the fastest-moving primates, and can swing through the trees at great speed. The swinging movement is called brachiation, and it allows gibbons to reach speeds of up to 56 kilometres an hour. This makes it practically impossible for any predator to catch a gibbon.

▲ Gibbons live in hot and humid rainforests in Southeast Asia. They make death-defying leaps between trees, covering up to 15 metres at a time, at great speed.

Silvery gibbons may look like monkeys, but they are actually apes. Apes are more similar to humans than monkeys – not just in appearance but in intelligence and behaviour too. Unlike monkeys, apes often stand or sit upright, they don't have tails, and their faces are flat. Gibbons are called 'lesser apes' while their cousins – chimps, bonobos, gorillas and orang-utans – are called 'great apes'.

4. Without stopping for a second,
the gibbon swings forward again.

3. The gibbon prepares
to grab the next branch with
its free hand.

**Gibbons spend all their lives
in trees and have long arms
and strong shoulders to
support their weight as they
swing through the trees.** They hold
onto one branch with one hand, then
swing forward as the other hand reaches
out to grab the next branch. Once they
get their speed up, gibbons can let go
between hand-holds and almost fly
through the trees.

Gibbons are light and agile. This allows
them to climb to the thinnest branches
and get food that other animals can't
reach. Gibbons make loud calls to one
another and their voices can carry for
distances of one kilometre or more.

I DON'T BELIEVE IT!

Gibbons' feet have
leathery soles and big
toes that can grasp onto
branches like thumbs.
Even so, gibbons
sometimes lose
their footing
and many fall,
suffering painful
broken bones.

Bonobos

▲ Bonobos stroke one another and clean each other's fur. This is called grooming and it's an important part of living as a group.

Bonobos are secretive apes and very little is known about them. For a long time, it was thought that they were a type of chimpanzee – but now they are recognized as a different animal altogether. They have smaller heads than chimps and long, lean limbs.

These black-faced apes are experts at talking to one another. They use their voices and their faces to tell each other exactly how they are feeling. The noises they make include hooting, barking and grunting. Bonobos even make a panting, laugh-like sound when they are playing or being tickled!

Baby bonobos depend on their mothers and stay close by them for the first few years of life. A newborn baby won't leave its mother's side for the first three months, and even when it is a year old, a young bonobo doesn't stray more than a few metres from its parent.

◄ Baby bonobos don't eat solid food until they are about one year old. Until then, they drink their mother's milk.

Being part of a family is very important to a bonobo. Young males always stay close to their mothers and never leave their group. Young females, however, eventually leave when they are about seven years old and join another group. Unusually, females lead the groups, not males.

ANIMAL GROUPS

Bonobos live in groups that are led by females. Use the Internet or a library to find out more about animals that live in groups. Investigate elephants, bees, penguins and lions.

Bonobos living in San Diego Zoo in America have been watched by scientists who want to find out more about how they behave. The scientists discovered that the bonobos invented their own game of 'blind man's bluff'. In this game, a young ape covers his eyes with his arm then tries to make his way through the play area without losing his balance or bumping into things. The others youngsters watch first, then join in the game!

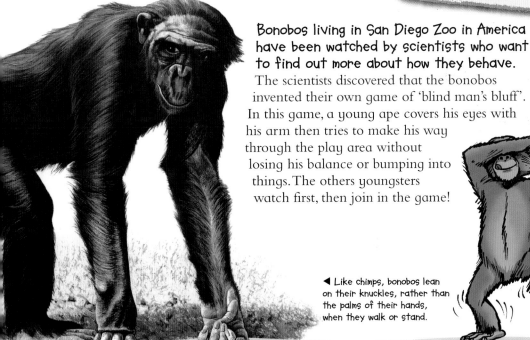

◄ Like chimps, bonobos lean on their knuckles, rather than the palms of their hands, when they walk or stand.

Clever chimps

Chimpanzees are our closest living relatives, yet they are in danger of extinction. It seems strange that humans don't do everything in their power to save the lives of their animal cousins, but chimps – the best known of all the great apes – are fighting a tough battle for survival.

Chimpanzees live in the rainforests of western and central Africa. They spend much of their time in trees, and they can swing from branches like gibbons, but not so well. When they are on the ground, chimps walk on all four limbs, and even run in this position. They can also stand up on their legs and can walk for up to one kilometre. Walking upright leaves their hands free for throwing stones at enemies, which they sometimes do!

◀ Not many animals are clever enough to use tools. This chimp is using a leaf to collect water.

Like most monkeys and apes, chimps eat plants and insects. They visit trees laden with fruit, when it's in season, but otherwise they eat flowers, seeds, nuts, eggs and honey. Unlike most other primates, chimps hunt other animals to eat. They also eat termites – small ant-like insects.

Termites live in large nests, so they can be difficult to reach. Chimps have worked out a way to get to the termites by using sticks. They poke the sticks into the termite nest and, once the bugs have swarmed all over the sticks, they pull them out and eat the termites.

▲ Chimps are 60 to 90 centimetres tall and weigh up to 60 kilograms. They spend a lot of time in trees, looking for food.

Chimps don't just use sticks to catch termites, they use them to pull down fruit from trees. They've also learnt how to use leaves to wipe down their bodies or to scoop up water to drink. Young chimps don't know how to do these things naturally – they only find out by watching adults and copying them.

◀ Chimps insert sticks into termite mounds to catch and eat the termites. Scientists have discovered that it is much harder than it looks!

QUIZ

Newborn apes are called 'babies' or 'young'. Can you match these animals to their young, which are given special names?

goat calf elephant caterpillar
butterfly foal horse kid

Answers:
goat – kid elephant – calf
butterfly – caterpillar horse – foal

203

Friend and foe

Chimps may look cute, but they can be very violent animals. They live in large groups and they defend their home area, or territory, from other groups. Young male chimps even patrol the edges of their territory, looking for intruders.

When male chimps come across strangers from other troops, they may attack them, even females. However chimps don't just attack other troops to defend their own territory – they will also invade other chimps' territories and kill them. In this way, a strong troop can take over the territory of a weaker one.

▶ An angry chimp is a terrifying sight. Male chimpanzees are amongst the most dangerous animals in the African rainforest. An adult male defending his territory may attack and kill chimps from other communities.

Chimps kill for food. They have been known to attack baboons, pigs and hoofed animals, such as antelope. Although a chimp may have some success when it hunts on its own, it's much better to be part of a hunting group. Adult chimps have been known to kill and eat young chimps – and there have even been some reports of chimps carrying off human babies.

Working together is easier if you can communicate with one another, and chimps are experts at communication. If one chimp finds some food it may hoot, scream and slap fallen tree trunks with its hands to get attention and bring others to the food. When chimps shriek or roar, the sound can travel up to one kilometre away!

Chimps don't just use noises to communicate, they also use facial expressions, kisses and panting. Chimps in captivity have been taught how to use sign language to communicate with humans. Sign language is a method of communication that mostly uses hands, rather than sounds, to show words and ideas.

When adult chimps from the same troop see one another they sometimes hug, and settle down to groom each other. Chimps use their fingers to run through each other's hair and pick out lice, dirt and twigs.

Orang-utans

The red apes of Sumatra and Borneo are called orang-utans and they are the only great apes that live in trees. These mighty animals are gentle creatures that spend most of their time alone, searching for food.

There are two different types of orang-utan. One lives on the Indonesian island of Borneo, and the other lives on the neighbouring island of Sumatra. Both types are in danger of extinction, but Sumatran orangs are not expected to survive the next 5 to 10 years.

Male orang-utans live alone. Some have their own territory, which they protect from other males. They have large cheek pads, big heads and masses of thick, long hair. At mating time they make loud calls that can be heard over long distances, telling the females to come and find them!

WHAT'S THE DIFFERENCE?

Male and female orang-utans look very different. Find out what the males and females of these animals look like:

Peacock   Fallow deer
Mallard duck

Despite their great size, orang-utans can climb trees, using all four limbs to grip onto branches. Once in the trees, they pick fruit, which makes up most of their diet. Although adults prefer to live alone, they will gather in groups around a fruit tree that is laden with ripe fruit.

◀ Young orang-utans stay with their mothers until they are about eight years old – longer than all other primates, except humans.

Sumatran orang-utans share their rainforests with tigers, clouded leopards and crocodiles. Small females and young orang-utans are more likely to be attacked by these deadly hunters than adult males are.

Gorillas

There are three types of gorilla – western, eastern and mountain – but they all look alike. These apes are the largest of all primates, and a mature adult male – called a silverback – can reach nearly 2 metres in height and weigh 200 kilograms.

Although there are three different types of gorilla, they all lead very similar lives. Gorillas live in forests – either tropical rainforests or rainforests in mountainous areas that can become cold. Mountain gorillas have longer, thicker fur to keep them warm. Gorillas eat plants and spend much of their day chewing leaves, shoots and stems.

At night, gorillas make themselves nests to sleep in. It only takes an adult about five minutes to break and bend twigs to create a good sleeping place. They never sleep in the same nest twice.

▲ Gorillas like to rest after every meal and at night. They make nests to sleep in up in trees. Large males make nests on the ground.

Gorillas are more likely to walk away from trouble than fight. If a family can't escape an intruder, the oldest male stares at the stranger, or barks. If this doesn't work, he stands up tall, hoots and beats his chest. He only runs at the intruder as a last resort – but he may use his huge fangs and considerable strength to kill his enemy.

◀ Gorillas live in groups. The silverback is the leader and protector of the group. He makes all of the day-to-day decisions.

QUIZ

1. What is the largest primate?
2. What is the smallest primate?
3. What is the name of the island where lemurs live?

Answers:
1. Gorilla 2. Mouse lemur 3. Madagascar

About two out of every five gorillas die before they reach their first birthday. Some are killed by silverbacks from other families, but scientists don't know the reason for most of the deaths. It's most likely that the babies simply become ill.

Primates at risk

Many monkeys, and all apes, are at risk of extinction. This means that once they die out, they'll be gone forever. There are different reasons for this, but the most important one is the loss of habitat. Humans are cutting down forests, woodlands and grasslands where primates live.

Orang-utans live in forests that are being cut down and turned into farmland to grow palm trees. The palm trees produce oil, which can be used in foods, to make soap and as a fuel for cars. Some of the forests are cut down for the wood that comes from the trees. Orang-utans are also hunted for meat by local workers.

◀ Large parts of the Earth's natural woodlands are being cut down. This is called 'deforestation'. The loss of their homes is the greatest threat to primates.

In Africa, gorillas and chimps are also dying out because their forests are being cut down. They have also suffered the effects of hunting over the last 200 years. At one time it was fashionable for Europeans to go to Africa, with the aim of killing as many animals as they could. Now poachers catch and kill gorillas and chimps to sell their body parts as souvenirs or for food.

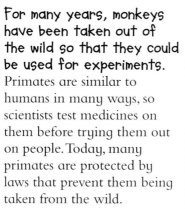

For many years, monkeys have been taken out of the wild so that they could be used for experiments. Primates are similar to humans in many ways, so scientists test medicines on them before trying them out on people. Today, many primates are protected by laws that prevent them being taken from the wild.

▶ A caged baby monkey in Thailand, which will probably be sold as a pet. Many primates are captured for experiments, or sold as pets.

There are around 700 mountain gorillas in the wild, only a few thousand Sumatran orang-utans and perhaps as little as 400 golden bamboo lemurs. The risk of extinction for most monkeys and apes is getting greater every year – and the outlook for them is bleak.

▲ Making animals perform for human entertainment is cruel and unnecessary. In parts of Asia, monkeys are trained to perform tricks to earn money for their owners.

I DON'T BELIEVE IT!

Every year, thousands of people all over the world dress up in gorilla costumes and run 7 kilometres to raise money to save the last wild mountain gorillas.

Bears

From polar bears to pandas, learn all
about bear behaviour and family life.

Habitats • Prehistoric bears • Cubs • Black bears
Polar bears • Brown bears • Hunting • Moon bears
Sloth bears • Spectacled bears • Sun bears
Giant pandas • Behaviour • Conservation

Masters of the forest

In the snowy lands surrounding the Arctic, bears used to be known as 'masters of the forest'. Bears are some of the largest creatures to live on land and they have few natural enemies, except humans. Once they roamed many of the planet's forests, but now these magnificent animals face an uncertain future.

▶ Brown bears eat a lot of fish and often wait at rivers and waterfalls for salmon. They catch the fish in their powerful jaws, or hook them out of the water with their huge paws, but they have to be quick!

What is a bear?

There are eight types, or species, of bear including polar bears, grizzly bears and giant pandas. All have large, heavy bodies, big heads and short, powerful legs.

Most bears are brown in colour. Polar bears have white, or yellow-white coats, which help them blend into their snowy Arctic habitat. Pandas have striking black-and-white markings. Bears have thick fur, which helps to keep them warm – and makes them look even bigger than they actually are.

▼ An angry bear may roar, opening its powerful jaw to reveal massive teeth.

When they show their teeth and growl, bears are a scary sight. They belong to a group of meat-eating creatures called carnivores. The large, sharp teeth at the front of their mouths are called canines, and they use them for stabbing and tearing at meat. These teeth may measure between 5 and 8 centimetres in length.

A close look at a bear reveals that its eyes are actually quite small compared to the size of its head. Bears have good eyesight, but their sense of smell is much stronger. They can even smell food hidden in a glove compartment, inside a locked car!

▶ A bear's paws and claws are fearsome weapons, but they are most often used for digging up food such as roots. The Malayan sun bear's long, curved claws make it an excellent climber.

I DON'T BELIEVE IT!

Bears may look like they rely on strength rather than speed to survive, but don't be fooled. Brown bears can run at nearly 50 kilometres an hour – much faster than most humans.

Bears use their teeth to defend themselves in fights and to hunt other animals. They have powerful paws to swipe at their attackers, and one blow can knock another animal to the ground. Their claws are long, knife-like, and reach up to 15 centimetres in length.

▼ A bear's skeleton helps to support its weight. The large skull protects the brain and the ribcage protects the internal organs.

Pelvis

Ribcage

Spine

Shoulder

Skull

Habits and homes

Today, most bear species are rare. They are still found in areas of the Arctic, the Americas, Europe and Asia, but once, bears lived in woodlands all over the world.

They may be carnivores, but bears are more likely to settle for a snack of leaves, roots and fruits than a meal of meat. The polar bear is the only bear that only eats meat, because there are almost no plants in the Arctic. Other bears rely on plants for the bulk of their diet, and since plants don't contain as much energy-rich fat as meat, bears have to spend lots of their time searching for food and eating.

▼ Bears like the sweet taste of ripe berries and feast on these in the autumn.

Bear life

Bears can live in a variety of places, from the icy north to the hot forests of South–east Asia. Sloth bears can even live in dry scrubland as long as ants and honey are available. Despite their size, most bears can climb trees.

▲ Brown bears spend the winter sleeping in rocky caves lined with leaves and grass.

Bears are solitary animals – they prefer to live alone. Mothers and cubs make small families, but once they have grown, young bears head off on their own to face the world by themselves.

Bears make the most of the summer and autumn months, when there is more food around, to eat and gain weight. When winter comes, bears that live in cool or cold climates retreat to their dens and sleep through the worst weather. They need big stores of body fat to help them survive during this time as they may not eat for many months.

▶ A bear family stays close together for safety. The cubs are at risk of being hunted by other meat eaters, including other bears.

Bears from the past

Arctodus **was the biggest bear to have ever lived.** It lived around the time of the last Ice Age, becoming extinct about 11,500 years ago. Known as the giant short-faced bear, it was over 3 metres in height when standing up on its back legs. The spectacled bears that live in South America today may be related to *Arctodus*.

◀ Fearsome *Arctodus* defends its kill from Ice Age wolves.

▲ Humans called Neanderthals hunted cave bears for meat, and used their bones and teeth as ornaments.

Meet my family

Who are your relatives — and where do you come from?

Ask your parents and grandparents about the people in your family, where they came from and what they did with their lives. There may be old family photos or letters you could look at together.

Cave bears were hunted by early humans, and this may have contributed to them dying out. They may also have found it hard to survive in the cold climate. The ground was covered in snow and ice for much of the year, and food would have been scarce.

Today's bears are thought to be descended from *Ursavus*, a bear that lived 20 to 15 million years ago. Also called the dawn bear, it was the size of a small dog, and lived in Europe when the climate was hot and humid, like today's tropics. It was millions of years before more bearlike creatures evolved.

Atlas bears were common in North Africa, until the Romans started capturing them in the 6th century. The bears, along with elephants and lions, were killed in arenas for entertainment. In a single day 100 bears could be killed, and numbers of wild Atlas bears fell dramatically. The last Atlas bears died around 140 years ago.

Giant cave bears were common in Europe during the Ice Age. Scientists have learnt about cave bears from the remains of teeth and bones they have found. They were similar to brown bears but were bigger and ate plants.

Curious cousins

There may only be eight species of bear, but other animals exist that are similar. In fact for many years, scientists thought that sloth bears were actually sloths (which is how they got their name) and that giant pandas were a type of raccoon! Some of these lookalikes are actually related to bears, but some just share their characteristics or life-style.

Bears are related to a family of animals called pinnipeds. These are mammals that live in the sea and come ashore mainly to breed. Examples of pinnipeds include seals, sea lions and walruses. Despite the fact that these creatures look completely different to bears, scientists have discovered that pinnipeds and bears probably shared a common ancestor, which lived around 30 million years ago.

▼ Their appearance and behaviour may be very different, but walruses probably share the same ancestor as bears.

◀ Red pandas look similar to raccoons, with bushy, striped tails, but they have red backs and black legs and bellies. They live similar lives to giant pandas, but are not bears.

Like giant pandas, red (lesser) pandas live in mountainous forests of China. They spend more time in trees than giant pandas and climb to escape predators or to sunbathe. They feed mainly on the ground, eating bamboo shoots, roots, fruit and small animals.

Bear cats are not bears or cats! Also known as binturongs, these stocky tree-climbers live in the tropical rainforests of south and south-eastern Asia. They have shaggy black fur and long gripping tails and will eat whatever food they can find, including fruit and birds.

Koalas are often called 'koala bears' but they are not related to bears at all. They are marsupials, which means they give birth to undeveloped young that are then protected in a pouch as they grow. Koalas only live in eastern Australia and feed on the leaves of eucalyptus trees.

▶ Koalas are similar to bears in appearance. They climb trees and have sharp claws.

Cute cubs

Female bears are called sows and they usually give birth to two or three babies called cubs. Sows start having cubs when they are four years old, and they may only have between eight and ten cubs in their whole lives. Adult males are called boars and they have nothing to do with rearing the youngsters.

▲ Newborn cubs are tiny and helpless. They have little or no hair, so they need to stay close to their mother for warmth. These grizzly bear cubs are just 10 days old.

They may have large parents, but bear cubs are very small. A giant panda cub weighs as little as 90 grams when it is born, and is easily hidden by its mother's paw. Cubs are born with their eyes and ears closed, and their bodies are either completely naked, or covered with a fine layer of soft fur. Like all mammals, female bears feed their young on milk, which is produced by the mother's body. For the first few months, cubs feed often and soon build up their strength.

Sows stay with their cubs and look after them for several years until they are old enough to fend for themselves. While they are with their mothers, cubs learn lots of skills, including how to find food and how to keep their fur clean. Mothers protect their cubs from predators, such as wolves or big cats, that may attack them.

Female bears give birth to their cubs in dens that they have prepared. They usually make their dens by digging into the soil, often under large stones or around tree roots. They line the den with dry plants and may use the same den for several winters. Polar bear mothers have to make their dens in snow and ice.

▶ Bears are mammals, like cats, dogs and humans, and females feed their young with milk that is produced by their bodies.

Black bears

Areas of North America and Canada are home to black bears. They live in mountains and forests, and despite being very shy, they sometimes stray into towns. They avoid brown bears, which also live in the American continent.

Most black bears are black, but some have brown or even white fur. Dark-furred black bears sometimes have lighter fur on their muzzles (noses) and chests. Their long, curved claws help them grip tree trunks when climbing trees.

TRUE OR FALSE?

1. A muzzle is the name given to some animals' long noses.
2. Black bears live in Europe.
3. 'Scavenge' means finding scraps and waste food.
4. A carnivore eats meat.

Answers:
1.True 2. False 3.True 4.True

These big bears need to eat plenty of food to keep their energy levels high. During the summer they mostly eat plants, but the actual food they eat depends on where they live, the time of the year and what is available. Black bears rarely hunt other animals, although they eat insects such as beetles, and love honey.

Black bears are regarded as the most intelligent of all bears. Those that live near humans often use their sense of smell to locate rubbish bins. They find ways to break into the bins and rifle through piles of garbage. Black bears are often found in national parks where they wander into campsites in search of food, particularly at night.

◄ Black bears avoid humans, and if they see people they are much more likely to run away or climb up a tree than attack.

Thousands of black bears are killed by humans every year. Only one out of every ten black bears dies naturally. The others are all killed by hunters, or after being hit by cars. Yet black bears manage to survive and are not in danger of becoming extinct.

Surviving the winter

Most black bears live in places where winters are very cold. This is a difficult time as food is scarce, and they survive by having a long winter sleep. This is called 'hibernating', and other bears that live in cold climates hibernate too.

▼ When snow and ice settle on the ground, black bears hide away. Female black bears look after their cubs in dens lined with grass and leaves.

During hibernation, a black bear's body systems slow down. Its body temperature drops and its heart beats much more slowly – dropping from 40 to 50 beats to just eight beats per minute! Unlike other hibernating animals, bears often wake up to clean themselves and get comfortable.

▲ Black bear cubs stay with their mothers for two to three years. A cub learns to hunt by watching and copying everything its mother does.

Pregnant females that are hibernating give birth in January or February. Sows look after their helpless cubs in their cosy dens until the spring arrives. They then leave their dens to hunt because after a long winter hibernating they are starving. During this time, sows prefer to eat meat rather than plants, as it is a good source of protein, so they can quickly build up their strength. They catch young animals that have been born in the spring, such as deer fawns, beaver kits and moose calves.

Some black bears have white fur! The kermode, or spirit, bear has a creamy-white coat and white claws, but is otherwise the same as an American black bear. They can have black or white cubs.

Black bears may spend most of the winter asleep, but they enjoy long naps in the summer too! They are most active in the early mornings and late evenings but during the hot daytime they often sneak under vegetation (plants) to sleep in the cooler shadows.

Polar bears

The polar bear is the biggest type of bear, and the largest meat-eating animal on Earth. These huge beasts have to fight to survive in one of the planet's bleakest places.

The Arctic is a snow-and-ice-covered region around the North Pole. Temperatures are record-breaking, dropping to an incredible −70°C and, unsurprisingly, very few living things are found there. Polar bears, however, manage to cope with howling winds, freezing snow blizzards and long winters.

I DON'T BELIEVE IT!

The word 'Arctic' comes from the Greek word 'Arkitos', which means country of the Great Bear. This doesn't refer to polar bears though, but to the Great Bear constellation, or pattern of stars, in the sky.

Polar bears are covered in a thick layer of white fur. This helps them to stay warm because it keeps in their body heat, and even absorbs some of the Sun's warming energy. Each hair is a colourless hollow tube which appears white when it reflects light. Some bears have yellow fur, especially in the summer when they spend less time in water and their coats get dirty.

Polar bears also have a layer of fat called blubber beneath the skin, which traps in heat. This is where the bears store energy for the months when they may not be able to find food. The blubber may be up to 12 centimetres thick and is so effective at helping the bear stay warm that polar bears are more likely to get too hot than too cold!

Female polar bears spend the winter months in dens so their cubs can be born safely. A mother spends five or six months in the snug den with her cubs, while the bad winter weather rages outside. She doesn't eat or drink during all of this time, but survives on her body fat.

◀ The Arctic summer is short, so polar bears like to soak up the sunshine in between hunting trips. Young cubs stay close to their mother at all times.

Life in the cold

The Arctic may be a difficult place in which to survive, but the seas and oceans around it are full of life. The huge number of fish attracts seals to these areas – and they are the main part of a polar bear's diet, especially ringed seals.

▶ Polar bears have been known to wait by a seal's breathing hole for hours, even days. When the time is right, they lunge forwards to catch their prey.

Unlike most other bears, polar bears don't have a home range (territory) that they stay in. The Arctic ice continually melts, refreezes and moves, changing the landscape throughout the year. Polar bears have to keep on the move and search for food. Their diets are 'fast and feast', meaning they may not eat for weeks, but when they find food they eat lots of it.

Seals are mammals and need to breathe air. They spend much of their time under water hunting fish, but they have to come up to the surface from time to time. Seals make themselves air holes in the ice and polar bears sit patiently, waiting for an unsuspecting seal to poke its head out of the water.

◀ A single swipe from a powerful polar bear's paw is enough to kill a seal.

With lightning reactions, a polar bear can lunge at a seal, whacking it with a powerful paw or grasping it in its enormous jaws. It then drags the seal away from the hole before tucking in. Polar bears have to spend around half their time hunting.

Polar bears are excellent swimmers and often take to the water to get from one iceberg to another. They can swim at speeds of 10 kilometres an hour using their paws to paddle through the crystal clear seas of the Arctic. They can dive underwater and hold their breath for up to 2 minutes.

Measure a bear

Polar bears are very big. They can measure over 3 metres in length. Use a measuring tape to see just how long this is. They can weigh nearly 800 kilograms – find out how many of you would weigh the same as one bear.

▼ Polar bears' bodies are well suited to the water. When a polar bear dives, its thick layer of body fat keeps it warm and its nostrils close against the icy water.

Brown bears

The mighty brown bear is a massive, shaggy-haired beast that lives in the northern parts of the world. Long ago, brown bears were spread far and wide across the world, but now they are finding it difficult to survive in places where they come into contact with humans.

Brown bears are now mostly found in forests, mountains and scrubland, in remote places where few people roam. There are brown bears in Northern Europe, Siberia, Asia, Alaska, Canada and parts of the United States. Bears from different areas can look quite different from one another. They vary in colour from yellowish to almost black.

Kodiak bears are the largest of all brown bears and can weigh up to 800 kilograms. They stand almost twice as high as a human. Their size is due to their diet – these big animals eat lots of fish, which is packed with healthy fats and proteins. Kodiak bears live on Kodiak Island, in Alaska, North America.

◀ A brown bear can reach 3 metres in length and normally weighs between 200 and 600 kilograms. They rub up against trees to scratch their backs.

I DON'T BELIEVE IT!

In Siberia, tigers and bears occasionally attack one another. However, a fight between the two animals is so evenly matched that they usually avoid one another!

Brown bears may be huge animals, but they can run with speed if they need to. Their walking looks slow and lumbering, but a scared bear can change pace very quickly – and run faster than most other animals.

Brown bears live in northern areas where it is very cold in winter, so they usually hibernate. Some types spend up to seven months in a den, but all bears wake up occasionally. When they wake they rearrange their bedding, clean themselves and return to sleep.

▶ Male bears are called boars and may sometimes fight one another using jaws, paws and claws.

Grizzlies are the famous brown bears of North America. They once roamed as far south as Mexico, but now they live in western Canada and Alaska. They get their name from the white hairs that grow in their brown coats, giving them a grizzled appearance.

Gone hunting

Grizzlies spend hours wading in water, or standing on a river's edge watching and waiting for salmon. During the summer and autumn, salmon swim upstream to lay their eggs, and as the fish swim past, the bears pounce on them.

▲ Grizzlies usually hunt and kill their prey, but they will also eat animal remains that have been abandoned by other hunters.

With a single blow from its large paw, a bear can easily stun a fish. Grizzlies can also catch their prey in their mouths, delivering a quick and fatal bite with their enormous teeth. Grizzlies are good swimmers, and will even dive underwater to catch salmon swimming past them.

Bears eat almost anything, from berries, shoots and roots to insects, fish and small mammals. Sometimes they hunt and attack living animals, especially young elks or caribou deer. They also eat carrion – the dead remains of animals killed by other predators, or hunters, such as wolves, coyotes and other bears.

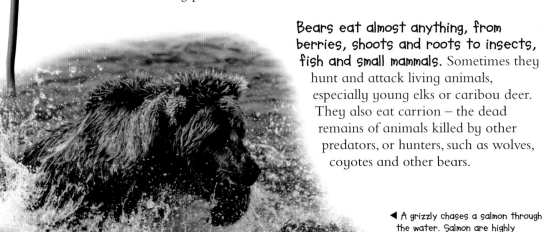

◀ A grizzly chases a salmon through the water. Salmon are highly nutritious, so brown bears that hunt them often grow bigger than other brown bears.

My Home

Do you know where you live? Ask a grown up to help you find your street on a map of your area, and then find your school. Can you trace the route home from your school, following the roads? Then use a big atlas and find your country on a map of the world.

▼ Grizzlies stand and wait for salmon to leap out of the water. Like other brown bears, they have distinctive humps on their shoulders.

Grizzlies may travel long distances in search of food, but they usually return to their territory. Bears are sometimes trapped and moved to other areas by scientists and wildlife managers to keep them away from humans, but a few have been able to find their way home – up to 200 kilometres away. No one knows how they do this, but their great sense of smell may help.

Grizzlies inspired the first teddy bear, which appeared around 100 years ago. Teddies were named after an American president called Teddy Roosevelt, who refused to shoot a grizzly on a hunting trip. The story was in a newspaper and a toyshop owner decided to make a stuffed bear – and called it a teddy.

237

Moon bears

Moon bears spend a lot of time in trees, sleeping or searching for nuts, leaves and fruit. They live in forested areas and are most active at night. Very little is known about how these animals behave in the wild.

These bears rely on their sense of smell more than sight or sound. They rub against trees, leaving a strong scent to warn other bears to stay out of their territory. Moon bears can be very aggressive if they encounter humans – they are more likely than an American black bear to kill a person, despite being smaller.

▲ Moon bears often eat farmers' crops such as maize (sweetcorn). They visit the fields and tear off the maize cobs using their long teeth called canines. This is why they are often trapped or hunted.

Moon bears are black bears of Asia and they have white or cream patches of fur on their chests. These patches of fur are often shaped like crescent moons – which is how they get their name. They are also known as Asiatic black bears.

I DON'T BELIEVE IT!

Moon bears build themselves nests up in trees, rather like birds! They make platforms from branches and plants and sleep in them at night, safe from danger.

▲ Some moon bears are kept in cramped cages so people can remove a fluid called bile that their bodies naturally create. Bile is an ingredient in some medicines. Many organizations are trying to bring this cruel practice to an end.

The moon bear can stand, and even walk, on its back feet. This skill led to many of these creatures being taken from the wild when they were still cubs. They were brought to circuses, where they were trained to 'dance' for the crowds.

Moon bears are threatened with extinction because their forests have been taken over by farmers. They are regarded as pests in many places, and many of them have been killed. In China, these bears are captured so their body parts can be used in traditional medicines.

◄ Moon bears weigh between 100 and 200 kilograms and measure up to 2 metres in length. Moon bears in captivity are able to stand up and beg for food.

Sloth bears

Sloth bears live in South-east Asia. They can survive in a variety of places, from forests to grasslands if they can find ants, termites and fruit to eat. A sloth bear's sense of smell is so good it can even sniff out ants in the soil beneath its feet.

▼ The claws of a sloth bear can measure 8 centimetres in length and are great for digging away at a giant termite mound.

When a sloth bear finds an insect nest it rips it open with its claws. They may tear the bark off a tree or dig into the ground. Once the nest is open the bear sucks up the insects. The sucking noise it makes can be heard up to 100 metres away!

◀ Sloth bears can give birth at any time of year, and the young are carried on the mother's back.

Sloth bear cubs can be born at any time of year, and there are normally one or two cubs in a litter. The mother protects the youngsters in her den until they are about three months old. When the cubs emerge, their mother carries them on her back until they are about nine months old.

▼ Using sloth bears as dancing bears is illegal, but it is thought that many cubs continue to be captured for this purpose. Ropes are forced through their noses and their teeth are removed. Wildlife organizations are campaigning to end this cruel practise.

Like other bear species, sloth bears are solitary animals, but they will sometimes gather together to share a big feast. A bees' nest full of honey or a large termite mound may attract two or more bears, but after the meal, they wander off on their own again.

When bears stand on their hind legs they get a better view of what's going on around them. Many bears do this, not just sloth bears. Standing on their hind legs helps them to sniff scents in the air, or to look larger and more dangerous when they are feeling threatened.

Spectacled bears

The spectacled bear has pale fur around its eyes, so it looks as if it's wearing spectacles! It faces extinction and may not survive this century.

Spectacled bears are relatively small, with dense black or dark brown coats. They spend much of their time in trees, where they sleep in nests built from branches. They are most active at night and are very shy, so not much is known about them.

Spectacled bears are skilled climbers. They use their long, sharp claws to grip onto tree bark as they clamber up a tree, and they sometimes make nests among the branches. They can also swim, but they don't eat fish. These bears travel around the forest on four legs, but mother bears can hold their cubs in their forelimbs, and walk upright on their back legs.

◀ Scientists can recognize individual spectacled bears from the markings on their faces — every bear has a different pattern of pale fur.

Farmers sometimes blame these bears for eating their animals, but this is unfair. Spectacled bears eat fruit, palms and bromeliads, which are plants that have stiff, spiny leaves. They can even eat cactus plants! They do occasionally eat small mammals, such as rodents, and insects.

Spectacled bears don't hibernate, because they live in warm places where this isn't necessary. Mother bears still build dens for their cubs, often in tree roots or under rocks. They make unusual noises to communicate with their cubs, including screeching and soft purring sounds.

▼ Spectacled bears are the only bears that live in South America. In mountainous regions such as Peru, they search for plants and small animals to eat. The males are about twice the size of the females.

Sun bears

The sun bear of South-east Asia may be the smallest of all bears, but it has the longest tongue – reaching up to 25 centimetres in length! A long tongue is very useful for reaching inside small cracks in trees and licking up tasty grubs and bugs.

▲ Sun bears are also called Malay bears, dog bears and honey bears. They have very short fur and yellow patches on their chests.

Apart from insects, sun bears like to eat birds, lizards, fruit, honey and rodents. Their jaws are so strong they can even crack open tough coconuts to get to the edible part inside. One of their favourite foods is honey, and sun bears use their very long, curved claws to rip open hives.

Sun bears are the smallest bears. They are nocturnal (active at night) and shy, so no one knows how many exist. They may be the most endangered bears. In Thailand, baby sun bears are popular pets – but once they grow up they are too dangerous, and are chained up or killed.

In the language of Malaysia, where some sun bears live, their name means 'he who likes to sit high'. It's a perfect name for these tree-loving beasts. A sun bear uses its strong muscles, the bare skin on the soles of its feet, and its long claws when clambering up trees, and these animals can spend many hours settled in the branches of a tree eating, sleeping and sunbathing.

Tigers and leopards hunt sun bears, but sometimes the bears wriggle free from these big cats' clutches. They have very loose, baggy skin on the backs of their necks, so if a predator attacks they can twist round and bite them!

▶ A sun bear will tear open a bees' nest with its claws before using its long tongue to reach the sweet honey. Its tongue can stretch 25 centimetres to lick food out of cracks.

Giant pandas

With its distinctive white face and black eye patches there are few animals that are as easy to recognize as the giant panda. These large bears have been brought to the brink of extinction, partly by human actions.

▼ Giant pandas only live in the cool bamboo woodlands and forests in China, South Asia. These areas are often covered in snow.

Pandas spend a lot of time on the ground, but they climb trees to rest or sleep. Youngsters first start climbing when they are just six months old and use their claws to help them grip onto the trees. Pandas like to rest in forked branches, and watch the world beneath them. They often come down from trees head first!

Pandas rarely eat meat, and spend around 16 hours a day chewing bamboo. This is a tough grass-like plant that grows very tall. Pandas also eat honey, eggs, fish, and occasionally mice.

▶ When they feed, giant pandas sit with their legs outstretched in front of them.

Pandas have a special bone on their wrists, which grows rather like a thumb. This bone enables pandas to grab hold of clumps of bamboo in their paws, making it easier for them to collect and eat their food. Pandas have to drink fresh water regularly, so they visit streams or rivers almost every day.

▶ Pandas' forepaws are bigger than their hind paws. The forepaw has a special pad of tough skin over an extra bone, which it uses like a thumb to help it grip bamboo.

Pandas are not ready to mate until they are about five years old. During the mating season males sometimes fight. Females usually give birth to one or two tiny cubs that are entirely helpless. Usually, a mother only feeds the first cub that is born and leaves the other one to die.

247

Under threat

It has been discovered that only about 1600 pandas live in the wild. This means that despite the efforts of Chinese wildlife workers, this species of bear may become extinct everywhere except zoos in the near future.

Pandas were only discovered by the western world in 1869 – but once people heard about them, they wanted to see pandas for themselves. The bears were captured, dead or alive, and brought to zoos or museums. We are still learning about pandas and only recently found out that males do headstands by trees to spray their urine high up to mark their territory!

Panda faces

You will need:
paper plate scissors
thick black paper glue string

1. With an adult's help cut a paper plate in half.
2. Cut out eye patches, ears and a nose from the black paper and glue them on to the plate.
3. Attach string to the back if you want to hang your panda face on the wall.

People have taken over pandas' habitats, forcing them into smaller, more remote mountainous areas. This means that less food is available to them. They are also slow breeders – females only produce about five to eight cubs in a lifetime, and these are vulnerable to attack by predators such as leopards, martens (weasel-like creatures) and Asian wild dogs.

Giant pandas spend up to 16 hours a day chomping and chewing on bamboo, and they often eat during the night too. They have to spend lots of time eating because their guts lack the bacteria that help other plant eaters, such as cows, get goodness from their food. From time to time, all the bamboo in one forest may flower and then die. The pandas in the area then face starvation.

◀ Every day, pandas eat between 10 and 20 kilograms of bamboo. They have the digestive systems of meat eaters, so they need to eat huge quantities of plant matter to get enough goodness to survive.

249

Myths and legends

Bears are seen as mighty, magical and majestic creatures in many cultures. They feature in folk tales and legends throughout the world, and are feared and respected in equal amounts.

Bears are sometimes thought of as powerful spirits that can influence peoples' lives. Long ago, people in northern countries feared a bear spirit could control other animals, and even take them away if they upset him.

Berserkirs were Viking warriors who dressed themselves in bear skins and worked themselves into a trance before battle. In this state, they were wild and fearless and dangerous to anyone who got in their way. This is where the word 'berserk' comes from.

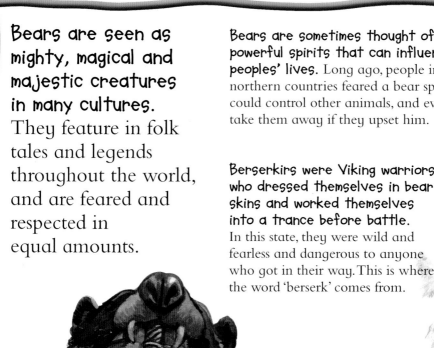

◀ Viking Berserkir warriors rushed madly into battle, wearing bear skins over their chain mail armour.

I DON'T BELIEVE IT!

Bears inspire people who want to be as strong as they are, so some sports teams are named after them. The Chicago Bears, for example, are an American football team and the Memphis Grizzlies are basketball players.

The Samoyed and Lapps are tribes of people who live close to the North Pole. Like other people who share their habitat with bears, they used to believe that, with the use of magic, humans could turn themselves into bears. Brave warriors were often thought to have taken on the spirits of bears as they fought.

◀ A Danish legend tells of a bear that was the king's ancestor. The bear was killed by dogs, but survives in folk tales.

A Danish story describes how a bear and a beautiful woman fell in love. The bear cared for her by stealing food from farms, until one day, farmers used dogs and spears to kill him. The woman later gave birth to a boy that looked normal, but was as strong and brave as a bear, who became the ancestor of the kings of Denmark.

▶ A giant armoured bear, called Iorek, features in the 2008 movie *The Golden Compass*, which is based on the book *Northern Lights*, by Philip Pullman.

251

Bear behaviour

Most bears are shy creatures and prefer to avoid coming into contact with humans. Mother bears, however, will attack any person or animal that comes too close to her cubs.

▶ When bears live near humans, they lose their fear of them and may even start to scavenge rubbish and other food.

CAUTION

ACTIVE BEARS IN AREA

PLEASE USE CAUTION WHILE WALKING:

- **CARRY A BELL**
- **MAKE NOISE**
- **BE ALERT**

Angry bears give warning signs that they may attack. These include making huffing noises, beating the ground with their paws or even making short charges. They may start growling, and their ears lie flat to their heads. Some bears do attack humans for food, but this is extremely rare – and they don't give any warning signs first. Running away from a bear just encourages them to start chasing.

Many grizzlies have learnt that they will find a free lunch wherever there are people. If grizzlies overcome their fear of humans they can become very dangerous. Once they have found a place where they can get food, they will return to it again and again.

◀ Being 'bear aware' can be a life-saver in some parts of the world. Bears are most dangerous when startled, so making plenty of noise when you're hiking in bear territory is one way of preventing an attack.

Dogs are being used in the Canadian Rocky Mountains to help train grizzlies to stay away from humans.
Troublesome bears that wander close to areas where there are lots of people are sedated with drugs that send them to sleep. When they wake up, the dogs bark and growl at them, chasing them away until they reach the safety of the woodlands. The bears quickly learn to stay away from houses!

American black bears are often feared by campers, but they rarely attack people.
In fact bears have much more reason to fear humans than we have to fear them. Around 30 to 40 people have been killed by black bears in the United States in the last 100 years, but 30,000 of these beautiful creatures are killed by humans every year.

Bear scare!

The advice if you see a bear up close is to slowly back away, watching it all the time. If the bear follows you, stand and wave your arms around while shouting loudly. The idea is to frighten the bear away, so you have to look as mean and angry as you can! Practise your angry face and shouting – you'll probably find it quite easy!

▶ A bear that was trapped near a town and examined by scientists as part of a study is chased away by a specially trained dog. This will keep it from returning to the area.

Big Cats

Explore the amazing world of big cats and
discover how these supreme hunters survive.

Tigers • Jaws and claws • Cheetahs
Pumas • Snow leopards • Senses • Fur and patterns
African grasslands • Cubs • Lions • Rainforests
Hunting • Leopards • Cat cousins

Cats – cute or killers?

All cats, big and small, are killers. Their bodies are perfectly designed to find, chase and kill animals. Unlike other hunters, such as dogs and bears, cats only eat meat. They are the supreme predators of the animal world and are amongst the most intelligent, beautiful, graceful and athletic of all creatures on our planet. While small cats have found a place in our hearts and our homes, big cats are trying to survive in a world that is taking away the space and freedom they need.

▼ The agile caracal lives in Africa and the Middle East. It hunts rats, hares, birds and baby mammals such as antelope and wild pigs.

Big, bigger, biggest!

All members of the cat family are mammals. They are all strong but swift and most can climb trees easily. Their faces are rounded and their muzzles short. Cats are predators, which means that they hunt other animals and their teeth are suitable for catching, killing and eating their prey. All cats have excellent eyesight.

▲ The Siberian tiger is covered with thick fur that keeps it warm during the winter months.

The tiger is not only the biggest cat it is also one of the largest carnivores, or meat eaters, living on land. Of all tigers, Siberian tigers are the biggest. They may weigh as much as 350 kilograms and can measure 3 metres in length.

MAKE A MONSTER CAT

You will need:
2 cups plain flour 1 cup salt
1 cup water varnish or paint
bowl spoon
1. Put the flour into a bowl. Add the salt and water.
2. Mix to form a smooth dough and mould into a cat shape.
3. Put your models onto a greased baking tray. Bake at gas mark 1 or 120°C for one to three hours. Once cool, paint or varnish your model.

▲ A jaguar's spots look like rosettes and often have a dark smudge in the centre.

The nimble cheetah does not need to be big to be successful. It has developed into one of the world's greatest predators, proving that skill and speed can make up for a lack of bulky muscles.

Sabre-toothed cats became extinct about 10,000 years ago. *Smilodon* was the most famous sabre-toothed cat. It was the size of a large lion and its canine teeth were a massive 25 centimetres long!

Jaguars are the biggest cats in the Americas. They measure up to 2.7 metres in length and can weigh an impressive 158 kilograms, which makes them the third largest big cat.

Lions hunt in groups called prides. This means that they can catch much larger animals than other big cats that hunt alone. By living and hunting together all the lions in the group eat regularly. Male lions usually eat first, even though the females do most of the hunting.

▲ *Smilodon* probably stabbed thick-skinned animals with its huge teeth.

Where in the world?

Big cats are found mainly in Africa, Eurasia and the Americas. Where an animal lives is called its habitat. Big cats have adapted to live in a wide range of habitats, from sun-baked deserts to the snow-covered forests of Siberia. Most big cats live in hot countries where there are plenty of animals for them to hunt.

▼ There are about 37 species, or types, of cat found in the world today. Most cats are solitary forest-dwellers.

NORTH AMERICA

▶ North, Central and South America are known as the New World. Jaguars, ocelots, margays and pumas, such as the one shown here, are all found in this area.

SOUTH AMERICA

Jaguars and pumas are cats of the Americas, or New World. While some jaguars are found in Central America, they have the best chance of surviving in the Amazon basin of Brazil. Here, the thick rainforest offers them protection from hunters. Pumas can live further north and south than any other species of large land mammal on Earth. They are found from the southernmost tip of Argentina, all the way north to Canada.

▲ The jaguar is best adapted to wetland habitats such as swamps and flooded forests.

◀ Tigers are only found in small regions of southern and eastern Asia. They live in a range of habitats, from tropical forests to Siberian woodlands.

The mighty tiger once roamed from south and Southeast Asia, all the way to the Russian Far East. Now it only survives in little pockets of land in these areas. Tigers have lost their habitat to humans who want to farm and live on the land that was once ruled by these huge animals.

ASIA

EUROPE

AFRICA

Millions of years ago the Americas were joined to Europe, Africa and Asia. The ancestors of modern cats were able to move across this huge landmass. But Australia, New Zealand and New Guinea separated from the other continents before cats appeared. That is why no cats are native to these places.

OCEANIA

▲ Cheetahs live in Africa and western Asia. Their habitat is open grasslands.

▲ Lions live in Africa. A small number, called Asiatic lions, survive in the Gir Forest of southern Asia.

Africa is home to many big cats including cheetahs, lions and leopards. Lions live on vast grasslands called the savannah. Their pale fur is the perfect colour to blend in with the dried grasses of the open plains. Cheetahs also hunt on the savannah, but tend to do so during the day, when the other big cats are resting.

261

King of the jungle

▶ Lions are often incorrectly referred to as 'Kings of the jungle'. However, it is tigers, not lions, that are at home in this environment. Tigers are endangered, which means that if we do not do enough to save them, they may soon become extinct.

The tiger is the largest of all the cats and also one of the hardest to find. Tigers live deep in the jungle where huge trees block out the sunlight, helping them to blend into the murky darkness. Their stripes camouflage them as they tread silently through the dappled shadows. This coat is also perfect for hiding the tiger in long grass.

Tigers hunt by stealth. They hunt at night, when they can creep up on their prey. Tigers may travel several kilometres each night, roaming along tracks, searching for their victims. Tigers hunt for deer, wild pigs, cattle, monkeys and reptiles. They will even kill young elephants or rhinoceroses.

Tigers love swimming. When it is hot they may take a dip in lakes and rivers to cool down. They are good swimmers and can make their way across large stretches of water.

Although they are powerful hunters, tigers may have to stalk 20 animals before they manage to catch just one. They normally kill once every five to six days and eat up to 40 kilograms of meat in one go! Tigers often return to a kill for several days until they have finished it, or scavengers have carried it away.

▼ People who need to go into the tigers' forest in Sundarban in east India and Bangladesh, wear masks on the back of their heads. This confuses the tigers into leaving them alone.

QUIZ
1. Why do tigers have stripes?
2. What name is given to animals that eat food that's been left by others?
3. If you were walking in a tiger's forest, how could you try to keep yourself safe?

Answers:
1. A stripy coat helps to camouflage them in the forest 2. Scavengers, e.g. hyenas and vultures 3. You could wear a mask on the back of your head

No two tigers have the same pattern on their coats. White tigers with black stripes are occasionally seen in the wild and are bred in zoos because they are very popular with visitors. Although they don't look like their parents, these tigers are not different in any other way.

▼ White tigers are rare in the wild. This white tiger cub is less likely to survive because its coat does not provide good camouflage.

Bengal tigers have a reputation as 'man-eaters'. Tigers don't usually eat people unless they are too sick or old to find other prey, but some tigers prefer the taste of human flesh. Between 1956 and 1983, more than 1500 people were killed by tigers in one region alone.

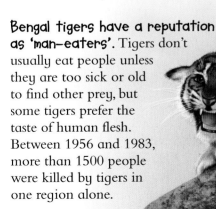

Jaws and claws

Animals have teeth that are best suited to the types of food they eat. Cats have long, sharp front teeth to bite and kill their prey. They also have strong back teeth to tear and chew pieces of meat.

Catching, killing and eating other animals is a tough job. In order to be successful hunters, cats need to have special teeth. Their pointy teeth are called canines. These are especially good for killing or holding onto prey. Behind the canines are carnassials. These teeth are ultra-sharp and they work like a pair of scissors to slice up flesh.

▼ This leopard has killed a gazelle. Leopards drag their prey up into trees where it is out of the reach of other hungry predators and scavengers.

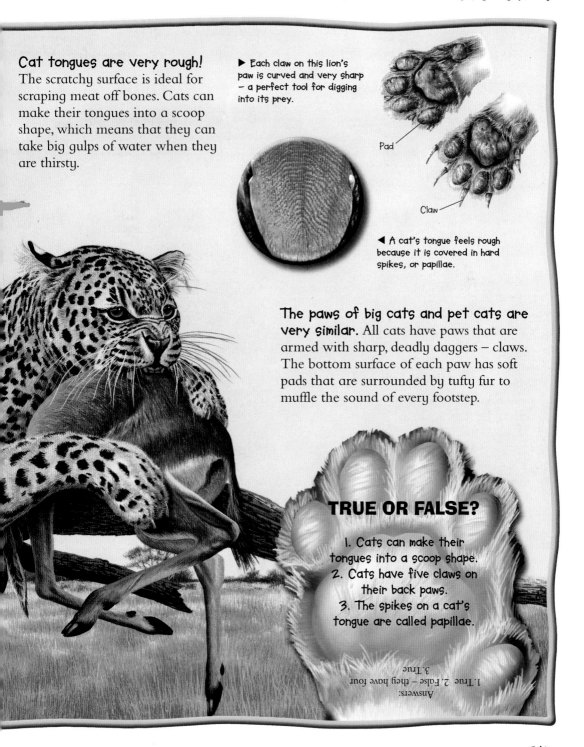

Cat tongues are very rough!

The scratchy surface is ideal for scraping meat off bones. Cats can make their tongues into a scoop shape, which means that they can take big gulps of water when they are thirsty.

► Each claw on this lion's paw is curved and very sharp – a perfect tool for digging into its prey.

Pad

Claw

◄ A cat's tongue feels rough because it is covered in hard spikes, or papillae.

The paws of big cats and pet cats are very similar. All cats have paws that are armed with sharp, deadly daggers – claws. The bottom surface of each paw has soft pads that are surrounded by tufty fur to muffle the sound of every footstep.

TRUE OR FALSE?

1. Cats can make their tongues into a scoop shape.
2. Cats have five claws on their back paws.
3. The spikes on a cat's tongue are called papillae.

Answers:
1. True 2. False – they have four 3. True

Going solo

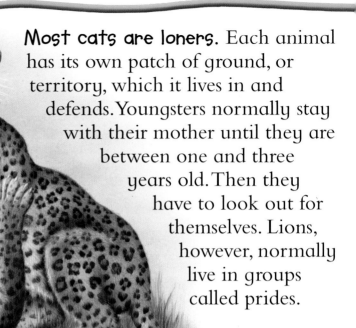

Most cats are loners. Each animal has its own patch of ground, or territory, which it lives in and defends. Youngsters normally stay with their mother until they are between one and three years old. Then they have to look out for themselves. Lions, however, normally live in groups called prides.

◀ A fight between two leopards over a territory can be extremely fierce and can even be a fight to the death.

I DON'T BELIEVE IT!

Young male lions get thrown out of the pride at about three years old, and spend their 'teenage' years roaming the plains, alone or with their brothers and cousins.

Lions live together. No one knows why lions live in groups. It may have something to do with their habitat. Hunting on the open grasslands might be easier in a group. Also, it's hard to hide your supper from scavengers, such as hyenas and vultures, when there are few bushes and trees. Maybe a group of lions can send a pack of nosy hyenas on their way more easily than a lion could on its own.

Cats mark their territory with their scent, which tells other cats to stay away. They do this by spraying urine on trees and bushes around their area. If another cat comes into their territory there may be a fight. Usually, big cats roar at intruders to scare them away rather than fight.

▶ By washing its face, this cheetah cub is putting scent from glands in its chin onto its paws. It can then mark its territory as it walks.

Cats' fur also carries a strong scent. Their scent is made by special parts of their body called glands. When cats wash they spread this smell all over their bodies, and as they rub against trees, the smell comes off. This is another way of marking their territory. That is why pet cats rub themselves against your legs – they are making it clear to other cats that you belong to them!

◀ Cats patrol their territories regularly. This jaguar is sniffing a tree to check that its scent is still strong.

Spotted sprinter

Cheetahs are the world's fastest land animals and can run as fast as a car. Within 2 seconds of starting a chase, a cheetah can reach speeds of 75 kilometres an hour, and it soon reaches a top speed of about 105 kilometres an hour. Cheetahs run out of energy after only 30 seconds of sprinting, so if its prey can keep out of the cheetah's jaws for this amount of time, it may escape capture.

This big cat lives in the grasslands and deserts of Africa and Middle East and Western Asia. Cheetahs do not often climb trees, as they have difficulty in getting down again. Cubs often hide in bushes so that they can surprise their prey. The word 'cheetah' means 'spotted wind' – the perfect name for this speedy sprinter.

▼ Cheetahs prefer wide open spaces where they can easily spot prey such as gazelles.

268

Like most of the big cats, cheetahs often live alone. Females live in an area called their 'home range', only leaving if food is scarce. When cubs leave their mothers they often stay together in small groups. Eventually the females go off to find their own home ranges, but the cubs may stay together and attack other cheetahs that come too close.

▶ Cheetah mothers keep their cubs hidden until they are old enough to start learning how to hunt.

Cubs have thick tufts of long, white fur on their heads, necks and shoulders. No one knows why they have this hair, but it might make them look bigger and stronger than they really are.

There are usually between four and six cubs in one litter. Sadly, only one cub in every 20 lives to be an adult cheetah. The others are usually killed by lions or hyenas.

Cheetahs kill antelopes by biting their throats, stopping them from getting any air. Cheetahs can spend a whole day eating if they are undisturbed by vultures or lions, which will steal the food if they can.

How fast are these animals?
Put them in order of fastest to slowest:
1. Cheetah 2. Kangaroo
3. Spur-winged goose
4. Thompson's gazelle

Answers: 1 3 4 2

Home on the range

Thousands of years ago, nearly half the world's land was covered in grasslands. Since then much of it has been built upon or turned into farmland. This has contributed to the falling numbers of big cats in these areas. Some grasslands are now protected. These places have become sanctuaries for wildlife.

Grasslands occur in places where it's too hot for trees, but there is enough rain to stop the land turning into desert. This is called the savannah and it is home to some of the most famous big cats. When it rains, the waterholes fill and the grass grows green. During the dry seasons, the Sun scorches the grass to the colour of sand and big cats struggle to find enough water and food to survive.

Grass is the favourite food of animals that graze. Animals such as giraffes, antelope and wildebeest nibble at the grass, or pick leaves off the bushes and trees that litter the plain.

I DON'T BELIEVE IT!
There are now only 12,000 cheetahs left in Africa, and no more than 200 in Western Asia. Many have been killed for their beautiful fur.

◄ Life in open grassland is difficult and dangerous for plant-eaters. There are few places to hide from hunters such as cheetahs and lions.

Zebra and other grazing animals make a tasty meal for lions and cheetahs. Since there are few trees to hide behind, it is difficult for these big cats to surprise their prey. Cheetahs rely on speed to catch other animals, while lions hunt in a group. These big cats watch a herd of zebra for some time before making their move. They try to spot any creature that is particularly small, weak or old. If they can separate this animal from the rest of the herd, it will be easier to kill.

Cub class

Cubs are born helpless and blind. A group of cubs is called a litter and there are usually between two and four in each one. Cubs depend on their mother's milk for the first few months of life, but gradually their mother will introduce them to titbits of meat that she brings back to the den.

▲ Lion cubs may stay with their mothers for two years or more before beginning an independent life.

▶ Mother cats such as this puma need to stay alert and on the lookout for danger. Their cubs, or kittens, make an easy target for other predators.

Male lions help to look after their young. When the lionesses are hunting, the males protect the cubs and play with them. When a hunt is successful the males eat before the females, but often let the cubs eat first. All lions have black tufts of fur on the ends of their tails. The tufts don't seem to have any use except as playthings for lion cubs!

▼ Lion cubs like to play. Even this tortoise is a source of interest. By playing like this, the cubs are learning hunting skills.

The babies of some cats, such as pumas, are called kittens. Adult pumas are sand-coloured to provide them with camouflage in the deserts and mountains where they live. Their kittens are born with spots on their fur that gradually fade. Spots are better camouflage for these youngsters, which hide in bushes and undergrowth.

Cubs learn how to hunt from watching their mothers. Many mother cats teach their babies how to hunt by bringing them small animals that they have captured alive. When they let the animal loose, the cubs or kittens can play with it and practise their hunting skills. It may seem cruel, but it is important that the cubs learn how to look after themselves.

I DON'T BELIEVE IT!

Cubs have a tough time making it to adulthood. Cubs are hidden by their mothers, partly to avoid bumping into any males. Male cats such as tigers kill any cubs that aren't their own.

273

Sociable simba

Lions are sociable animals. They live in family groups called prides that normally include between four and six adults, all related, and their cubs. Large prides of perhaps 30 animals develop where there is plenty of food.

The best time to hunt is early morning or evening. The lionesses prepare an ambush by spreading out and circling their prey. They hunt zebra, wildebeest, impala and buffalo. A group of lionesses has been known to bring down an adult giraffe that was 6 metres tall!

▶ Lionesses give birth to a litter of between one and six cubs. The cubs stay with their mother for over two years.

Unlike other big cats, male and female lions look very different. They both have sandy-coloured fur that blends into sun-scorched grasslands, but the males have manes of darker hair on their heads and shoulders that make them look powerful and threatening.

Although it is unusual, lions do sometimes attack and eat humans. In the 1930s and 1940s, a family of lions in Tanzania preferred human flesh to the normal lion diet of antelope. They killed nearly 1500 people in just 15 years.

I DON'T BELIEVE IT!
Every cat's favourite pastime is napping. Lions spend almost 80 percent of their time sleeping, lying down or sitting doing nothing!

Adult males only stay with their pride for a few years at a time. If a male wants to become the leader of another pride, it must fight the males and kill the cubs. This seems very cruel, but it does this to make the lionesses ready to have more cubs before it mates with them. The new leader then knows that all the cubs in the pride will be their own.

Few animals would dare to attack a healthy lion. When a lion has become old and weak, however, it may be easy prey for a band of hyenas. It is said that lions only fear hyenas — this is because they know they could end up in the bellies of several of them!

275

Jungle cats

More than half of the world's wild cats live in forests and jungles. In some of these forests, the weather remains hot and wet all year round. In others there are long dry spells, followed by periods of heavy rain. These rainy seasons are known as monsoons. Both types of forest are packed full of animal and plant life.

◀ Jaguars live in South American rainforests, but often stray onto farmland and prey on domestic cattle.

276

▲ Tigers prefer wet habitats and they are strong swimmers.

Tigers hide in tall grass and thick vegetation. As the sunlight and shadows flicker on the tiger's stripy fur, it blends into the background. It moves little during the day and spends most of its time resting. As the sun fades, it creeps through the forest, its paws softly padding across the forest floor. It is looking and listening for any animal that it may catch unawares.

Some jungle areas are protected and people are not allowed to cut down the trees. These areas are called 'reserves' and are meant to provide a place where animals, including all kinds of big cats, can live safely in peace.

Leopards are skilful hunters. Despite this, they are becoming increasingly rare in rainforest areas due to the destruction of their habitat.

QUIZ

Look at this list of jungle animals and decide whether each is a bird, mammal or reptile:
1. Toucan   2. Python
3. Gibbon   4. Vulture
5. Margay   6. Turtle

Answers:
Birds: toucan and vulture
Mammals: gibbon and margay
Reptiles: turtle and python

Swift and sure

Big cats move in a similar way to smaller cats. They are very athletic and are able to run, climb, pounce and leap almost silently. These skills are important because when hunting they need to get as close to their prey as they can before attacking it.

▼ All cats run in a similar way. They push off with both hind legs together but land on one front foot and then the other.

Domestic cat

Cheetah

Can you link each bone to its important job?

1. Skull 2. Ribs 3. Spine

a) Contains the nerves
b) Protects the heart
c) Protects the brain

Answers:
1.c 2.b 3.a

Cheetahs are the fastest of all cats. Their spines, or backbones, are so bendy they can bring their hind legs forward between their front paws when they run. This means that they can take huge steps as they bound forwards. Unlike most cats, they do not have retractable claws on their feet. When they run their claws stick into the ground like the spikes on an athlete's shoes.

Some cats, such as leopards, spend a lot of their time in trees. Long tails help them to keep their balance as they move along narrow branches. They can chase monkeys high up into a tree, keeping their footing on branches that seem too flimsy to support a squirrel! If the monkey falls the leopard will turn and race headfirst down the tree to reach its prey.

1. The caracal may lose its footing as it chases prey along branches

▶ When tree-climbing cats like caracals fall from a height they can usually regain their balance and land on their feet.

2. It has a superb sense of balance and quickly begins to right itself

3. A flexible spine helps the falling caracal twist its body

4. Cats' muscles are very strong and their joints are very flexible so the caracal can absorb the shock of hitting the ground to give it a 'soft landing'

Do cats really have nine lives?

It often seems that cats can survive almost any scrape they get themselves into. They don't have nine lives but their strength and quick reactions can save their lives. When a cat falls out of a tree, it can twist its body round so that it lands on its feet – and walk away with its head held high and a flick of its tail!

American athlete

▲ Pumas live in the New World, from the southern tip of South America all the way to Alaska.

The puma is a great athlete. Pumas have long hind legs packed with muscles — ideal for jumping, running and climbing. Of all the big cats, these are the most graceful. They can spring 2 metres into a tree then bound up a further 18 metres before leaping down to the ground.

Pumas are known by a variety of names including cougar, panther, red jaguar, mountain screamer, catamount, deer tiger and mountain lion. People from Central and South America call them *chimblea*, *miztil*, *pagi* or *leopardo*.

I DON'T BELIEVE IT!
Though large in size, the puma is not one of the seven species of 'big cats' so it cannot roar. Instead, it makes an ear-piercing scream which scares both humans and animals alike!

Scr e eeech!

When you live in a hot climate and are covered in a coat of fur, it can be difficult to keep cool. Pumas, like other cats, pant to lose heat. When an animal pants, it opens its mouth and lets its tongue hang out. This means that water can evaporate off the surface of the tongue, lowering the animal's body temperature.

Rabbits, mice, rats and hares are popular prey for pumas. They will also attack larger mammals, including deer, cattle and elks. In some places, humans have built houses in or near the pumas' natural habitat. This has resulted in people being attacked – even killed – by these wild animals. Now, people are beginning to realize that they have to respect the pumas' natural instincts and stay away from their territory.

These big cats are highly skilled killers. They hunt by slowly creeping up on an unsuspecting victim. When ready, they pounce, knocking their prey to the ground in one sudden hit. A single, swift bite kills the puma's victim immediately.

▼ Pumas often hunt small animals, such as hares, squirrels, beavers and turkeys.

Although pumas can kill porcupines, it is not an easy task. They need to flip the prickly creature onto its back before biting its soft belly. If the porcupine manages to spear the puma with one of its many spines, the wound may prove fatal.

◀ The North American porcupine can climb trees and has a crest of long spines, or quills, on its head and back.

Life in a cold climate

There are no wild cats living in the Antarctic. Maybe the weather is too cold for them or there are too few animals to eat. Some big cats do live in cold climates. Like all animals that live in these remote areas, they grow thick fur and store extra layers of fat under their skin to keep warm.

The beautiful snow leopard lives in one of the most challenging habitats in the world. It roams a mountainous area of Central Asia where the weather is cold and few plants are able to grow. Snow leopards live alone and travel across a huge area searching for food.

I DON'T BELIEVE IT!

While Siberian tigers survive winters at temperatures as low as −33°C, the Bengal tigers try to keep cool in hot forests where temperatures can reach a sweltering 38°C!

Snow leopards hunt yaks, asses, sheep and goats as well as smaller mammals and birds. They survive the extreme cold because they have very thick fur, especially in winter. They also wrap their long tails around their bodies when they sleep to keep in heat. A snow leopard's grey coat helps to camouflage it in snow. During the summer, snow leopards often take a dip in mountain streams to cool themselves down.

Siberian tigers live in cold climates in Russia and China. Their coats are pale with brown stripes, rather than the more common black stripes. During the winter months their fur grows long, thick and shaggy to help keep them warm. They hunt other creatures that live in this harsh climate, such as wild boar, moose, sika deer and bears.

▼ Despite its name the snow leopard is quite different from other leopards. It is smaller and its coat is much paler and thicker.

Super senses

▼ Cats have eyes on the front of their heads. Eyes in this position are best placed for judging distance. This jaguar has fantastic night vision but its colour vision is not as good as ours.

▲ Cats' eyes appear to glow in the dark because they have a layer of cells that reflect light.

At night, cats can see four times better than humans. This is because they have a layer at the back of the eye that reflects light. This helps cats to see things clearly in low light.

All cats have flexible ears that they can turn towards any sounds they hear. Cats also use their ears to show how they are feeling. An angry cat will lower and twist its ears so that they are lying almost flat against its head.

Cats sniff their food before eating to check it is not bad or poisonous. They also sniff the bushes and trees in their territories to discover if any other animals have passed by.

▶ Clouded leopards use their whiskers to help them find their way through dense jungle vegetation, especially at night.

A cat's whiskers are special hairs that are extra-sensitive.

They are particularly useful at night when it is likely to be hunting. As the cat moves through undergrowth, its whiskers brush against the leaves, helping it choose a safe path. It is only by using all of their senses together that cats are able to move about easily in darkness.

▼ Despite their doglike appearance hyenas are more closely related to cats than dogs.

Cats use all of their senses to stay alive.

As hunters, they need to be able to find, chase and catch their prey. Although big cats do not have many natural enemies, they need to watch out for scavengers, such as hyenas. These animals gang up on big cats and steal their meals.

A coat to die for

The jaguar is the owner of a beautiful fur coat — so beautiful that many people want to own it too. Although it is against the law to capture a jaguar for its skin, they are still hunted. Jaguars live in rainforests, often in areas where farmers are cutting back trees to grow crops. As jaguars' habitats continue to shrink, so will their numbers.

Of all the big cats jaguars are the most water-loving. They like swampy areas, or places that flood during wet seasons. Jaguars are strong swimmers and seem to enjoy bathing in rivers. They live in Central and South America but less than a hundred years ago, they were living as far north as California and Texas.

▼ Jaguars are similar to leopards but they have broader shoulders, shorter legs and larger heads. All jaguars love water.

At first glance a jaguar looks like a leopard, but it is possible to tell them apart by a few tell-tale differences. A jaguar's head is bigger and rounder than a leopard's, with round ears not pointed ones. Its tail is quite a bit shorter than the leopards and its shoulders are broad and packed with muscle.

Young jaguars climb trees where they hunt for birds and small mammals. As they grow bigger they become too heavy for the branches. Adults tend to stay on the ground, or in water, to hunt.

▲ A capybara's eyes, ears and nose are on the top of its head so that it can spot a lurking predator as it wallows in water.

Jaguars hunt a wide range of animals including deer, tapirs, birds, fish and capybaras. Capybaras are the world's heaviest rodent and can measure up to 130 centimetres in length.

▶ Jaguars can feed on turtles because they have large, heavy teeth and immensely powerful jaws.

I DON'T BELIEVE IT!

In one year alone, at least 13,500 jaguars were killed for their coats. Today, the future of the jaguar is most at risk from the destruction of its rainforest habitat.

Jaguars' powerful jaws are so strong that they can crack open the hard shells of turtles and tortoises. These cats will even kill large animals, such as cattle and horses. It is their habit of killing cows that upsets many people who share the jaguars' territory. Cattle are very important to the farmers, who may poison or shoot jaguars that are killing their livestock.

Spots and stripes

Tiger fur

Cheetah fur

▲ The top layer of a cat's coat is made of coarse, long hair. It is this hair that is coloured and carries the pattern.

Patterned fur has helped cats survive, but it may be the death of them. For centuries, people have hunted cats for their beautiful coats. In some cases this has brought big cats to the edge of extinction.

A cat's fur keeps it warm when the weather is cold and cool when it is too hot. The fur is made up of two layers – a short and fluffy bottom layer and a top layer that is made of longer coloured fur.

▼ No one really knows why a lion's coat is generally plain tawny, while cheetahs and leopards, which live in similar habitats in Africa, are spotted. This lion's coat enables it to almost disappear into the long grass.

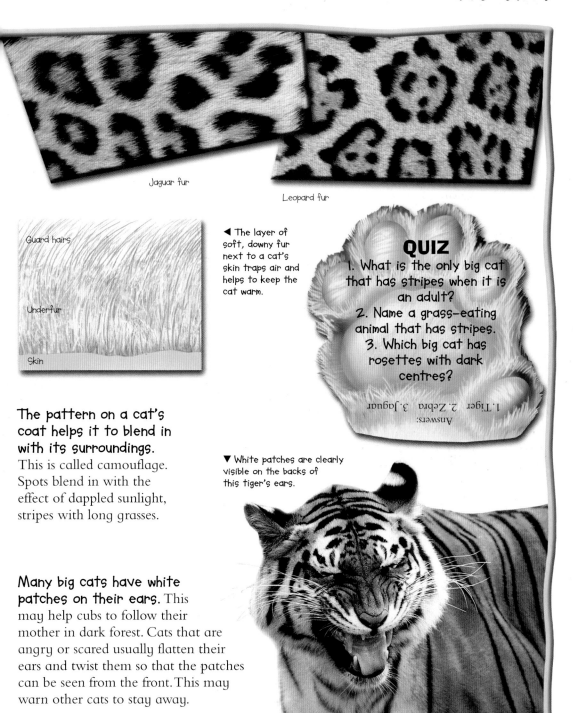

Jaguar fur

Leopard fur

Guard hairs

Underfur

Skin

◀ The layer of soft, downy fur next to a cat's skin traps air and helps to keep the cat warm.

QUIZ
1. What is the only big cat that has stripes when it is an adult?
2. Name a grass-eating animal that has stripes.
3. Which big cat has rosettes with dark centres?

Answers:
1. Tiger 2. Zebra 3. Jaguar

The pattern on a cat's coat helps it to blend in with its surroundings. This is called camouflage. Spots blend in with the effect of dappled sunlight, stripes with long grasses.

▼ White patches are clearly visible on the backs of this tiger's ears.

Many big cats have white patches on their ears. This may help cubs to follow their mother in dark forest. Cats that are angry or scared usually flatten their ears and twist them so that the patches can be seen from the front. This may warn other cats to stay away.

Supercat

▲ There are probably more leopards in the wild than all the other big cats put together. This success has earned leopards the nickname 'supercat'.

Leopards can live close to humans but never be seen by them. They live in Africa and as far east as Malaysia, China and Korea. Leopards hunt by night and sleep in the day. They are possibly the most common of all the big cats, but are rarely seen in the wild.

Leopards may sit in the branches of a tree, waiting patiently for their meal to come to them. As their prey strolls past, the leopard drops from the branches and silently, quickly, kills its victim.

Leopards nearly always hunt at night. A leopard approaches its prey in absolute silence, making sure that it does not snap a twig or rustle leaves. With incredible control, it places its hind paws onto the exact places where its forepaws had safely rested. When it is within striking distance of its victim it will attack.

Leopards are not fussy eaters. They will eat dung beetles, frogs or birds if nothing better comes along. They prefer to hunt monkeys, pigs and antelopes.

◄ Dung beetles feed on dung and lay their eggs in it. They make a crunchy snack for hungry leopards.

Once a leopard has caught its meal, it does not want to lose it to passing scavengers such as hyenas or jackals. The leopard might climb up a tree, hauling its prey with it. It may choose to eat immediately or store the animal for later. Hiding food like this is called 'caching' (known as 'cashing').

Although the name 'panther' is usually given to pumas, it is also used for leopards that have black fur. Black panthers are not a different type of leopard – some cubs are simply born with black fur rather than the normal tawny-brown hide.

◄ If you could get close enough to a black panther you would see that its fur is spotted.

Scaredy cat

The world's most mysterious cat is the clouded leopard. It is very shy and very rare. In fact, it is difficult to say how many of these pretty creatures are alive today, it is so unusual to even spot one! It is about 2 metres in length, half of which is its tail, which it uses to help balance in the trees.

Clouded leopards are excellent climbers and live in the forests of Southeast Asia, from Nepal to southern China. As it was once believed that they spent most of their time in trees, they were given the name 'tree cats' in Malaysia. Scientists studying them now think that they also live in grassland and mangrove swamps, and spend at least as much time on the ground as they do in the trees. Clouded leopards eat wild boar, monkeys and deer, which they catch by stalking.

The clouded leopard is a big cat that behaves like a little cat! It can jump around in trees as easily as a domestic tabby. These agile animals have been seen running headfirst down a tree trunk and even hanging upside-down by their hind feet. If that isn't enough, these gymnasts like swimming too!

I DON'T BELIEVE IT!
Clouded leopards can leap distances of more than 5 metres as they clamber through the treetops of their forest home.

◀ Little is known about clouded leopards. They sleep all day and only hunt at night. Despite their length, these cats weigh only about 20 kilograms – roughly the same as a six-year-old child.

While no one knows how many clouded leopards there are left in the wild, experts agree that their numbers are declining. This is partly because their habitat is being destroyed, but they are also being hunted for their fur. Their teeth and bones are used in traditional Asian medicines. Sadly, clouded leopards do not live happily in zoos either, rarely breeding in captivity.

293

Cat cousins

▼ The African serval often hunts water voles in the reeds and rushes that surround lakes and waterholes.

Several types of small wild cat live around the world. There are about 37 types, or species, of cat — big and small. Added to this there are 300 breeds of domestic (pet) cat. Whether they are big or small, all cats are natural-born predators.

One of the world's bounciest cats is the serval. It can leap one metre high and travel a distance of 4 metres as it jumps like a jack-in-the-box to strike at its prey. All this effort may be for a small supper of frogs or locusts, which are some of the serval's favourite titbits.

The serval is unusual because it hunts during the day. Most cats prefer to hunt at night or during the dimly-lit hours of morning or evening. Servals live in the African savannah and look very similar to cheetahs, with a slim, graceful body and long, slender forelimbs.

Like its neighbour the jaguar the ocelot has been hunted for its fur. It lives in the forests, grasslands and swamps of South America. Ocelots usually live alone or in pairs and will eat almost anything they can catch. Until the hunting of these extraordinary cats was made illegal, as many as 200,000 pelts (skins) were sold every year.

▶ The ocelot is extremely agile and can leap from the ground on a dark night and grab a low-flying bat in its paws or mouth.

One super-springy cat is the caracal. It can leap an astonishing 3 metres into the air to swipe at a passing bird! A long time ago, this fine hunter was trained to catch birds and hares in India and Iran. Caracals live in dry, scrubby habitats which is why it has another name: the desert lynx.

The lynx can change its coat according to the weather. In fact its winter coat looks so different from its summer one that you might not think it was the same animal! This cat lives in pine forests across northern Europe and Asia. All year round, it has a short tail and tufts of fur on the tip of each ear. It can kill animals four times bigger than itself.

◀ Wide, furry paws help prevent a lynx from sinking into the snow and give it a good grip on icy rocks.

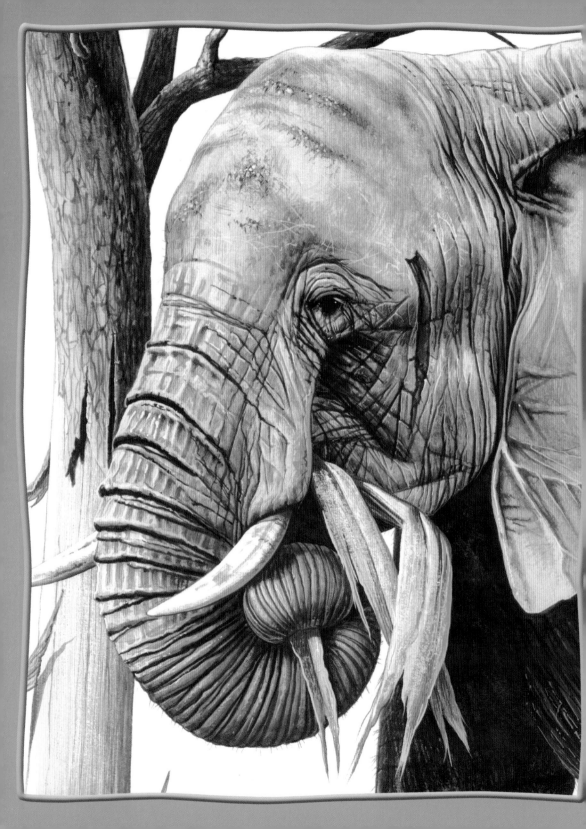

Elephants

Get an insight into the lives of the largest
land-living animals on Earth. Find out how
elephants raise their young and find food.

Elephant ancestors • Homes • Trunks
Teeth and tusks • Food • Babies • Bulls
Communication • Intelligence • Ivory
Working elephants • Conservation

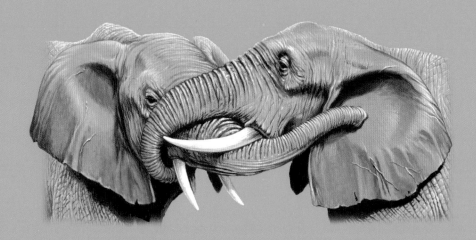

Gentle giants

Elephants are amazing creatures. They are bigger than any other animals that live on land, yet their closest living relatives are no larger than rabbits. Elephants are powerful, but they are also sensitive, intelligent creatures that live in close, caring families. They are strong enough to topple a tree, but gentle enough to pick a flower with their trunks. These mighty beasts have been part of human history for centuries, but now they face an uncertain future.

▶ African savannah elephants walk slowly across the grassy plains. They live in close family groups called herds and spend most of their time eating and searching for food.

Elephant ancestors

Elephants belong to an ancient family of animals that had long noses, or trunks. Members of this family, called palaeomastodons, have become extinct (died out) except for three – African forest and savannah elephants and Asian elephants.

One of the elephant's relatives looked like a pig with a long snout. This odd-looking creature is called *Moeritherium*. It lived between 50 to 35 million years ago.

▼ Palaeomastodons lived around 35–40 million years ago in North Africa. They are the possible ancestors of modern elephants.

Moeritherium lived 50 million years ago

Scientists know what extinct animals looked like by studying fossils. These are the remains of dead animals and other living things that turned into stone over millions of years. Usually, just hard parts, such as bones and teeth, survive as fossils.

The remains of woolly mammoths have been found in blocks of ice. These animals were relatives of modern elephants that became extinct about 10,000 years ago. Because the remains have never thawed out, they have been preserved in the ice.

◄ Woolly mammoths had thick, shaggy fur to keep them warm, small ears and enormous tusks.

Primelephas lived
7 million years ago

People hunted mammoths for food and fur. Humans and mammoths lived in the Ice Age, when food was scarce. By working in groups to find, chase and kill mammoths and other animals, humans were able to survive this tough time.

▼ Columbian mammoths lived in North America, where the climate was less cold. Their bones, teeth and tusks have been found preserved in rock.

Palaeomastodon lived
35 million years ago

I DON'T BELIEVE IT!

Mammoths preserved in rocks or ice probably died quickly. They may have fallen into lakes that froze, or got swept away in rivers before their bodies could be covered in mud and rot away.

Not all mammoths were woolly. The earliest ones lived more than four million years ago in grasslands. Here, the weather was warm so they didn't need thick fur. Mammoths were a very successful group of animals, and they lived in many parts of the world, probably in their millions.

Curious cousins

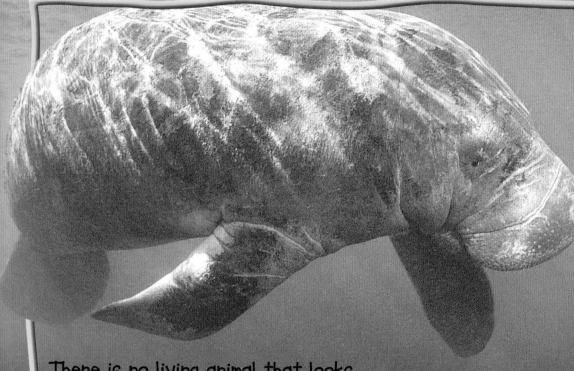

There is no living animal that looks like an elephant. To find out who their closest relatives are, scientists use clues, such as the type of teeth and bones that animals have. They have discovered that elephants have some strange relatives.

▲ Where there is plenty of food, manatees may live in groups of up to 100 animals.

Dugongs are huge, sea-dwelling animals. It is hard to believe that they are the closest living relatives of the elephant, but they share the same ancient ancestors. Dugongs eat plants underwater and come to the surface to breathe air.

Manatees, also known as sea cows, look similar to dugongs. They are also related to elephants. Manatees live along coasts and in fresh water, particularly in marshy areas, where they graze on plants. They can grow to over 4 metres long.

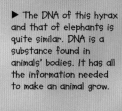

▶ The DNA of this hyrax and that of elephants is quite similar. DNA is a substance found in animals' bodies. It has all the information needed to make an animal grow.

QUIZ

a. Dugongs and manatees live in the water.
True or false?
b. Aardvarks are friendly animals that are easy to spot.
True or false?
c. Hyraxes have beaks instead of teeth.
True or false?

Answers:
a. True b. False c. False

Hyraxes may be the size of a rabbit, but they are the elephant's closest living relative. The bones in their feet are similar to the elephant's, and they have tusk-like teeth that keep growing all their lives. These little mammals eat plants and live in Africa and the Middle East.

Aardvarks live in Africa, but they are so shy that little is known about them. They live alone in burrows, only coming out at night to search for their favourite food of ants and termites. They probably had the same ancestor as elephants, many millions of years ago.

▼ Aardvarks bear little resemblence to elephants, but scientists believe the two are related.

Elephant shrews, tenrecs and golden moles may also be part of the elephant's wider family. Elephant shrews are small African mammals that eat insects. Tenrecs live in Africa, and Madagascar. They have long snouts that are covered in sensitive hairs and eat insects, worms and grubs. Golden moles are rarely seen as they spend most of their lives in underground burrows.

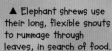

▲ Elephant shrews use their long, flexible snouts to rummage through leaves, in search of food.

Where in the world?

There are three main types of elephant — two African and one Asian. African elephants are larger and they can measure up to 5 metres in length. Both males and females have tusks, which are long teeth that grow out of the mouth on either side of the trunk. They only live in Africa, but they are found in many types of habitat.

▶ African savannah elephants have huge ears and long, curved tusks.

There are two types of African elephant — forest and savannah.
Forest elephants have darker skin than those that live on the savannah. They also have yellow-brown tusks that point downwards rather than curve upwards, and their trunks can be quite hairy. Forest elephants live in areas where there is a lot of thick vegetation.

▲ Asian elephants usually have smaller tusks than their African cousins, and much smaller ears.

Asian elephants are found in India and other parts of Southeast Asia. Males can weigh over 5 tonnes and measure more than 3 metres from the toe to the shoulder. Female Asian elephants do not always have visible tusks and are smaller than the males. The teeth of Asian elephants are very like those of mammoths, and it is thought that these two animals are closely related.

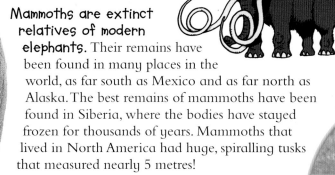

Mammoths are extinct relatives of modern elephants. Their remains have been found in many places in the world, as far south as Mexico and as far north as Alaska. The best remains of mammoths have been found in Siberia, where the bodies have stayed frozen for thousands of years. Mammoths that lived in North America had huge, spiralling tusks that measured nearly 5 metres!

▼ Asian elephants have been used for farming and carrying loads for centuries. Like all elephants, they enjoy soaking in water.

▼ Most African elephants live on the savannah (huge grasslands) although they can also survive in mountains, deserts and forests.

ASIA

AFRICA

◄ The ears of a forest elephant are slightly smaller and more rounded than those of a savannah elephant.

What a handy nose!

No animal on the planet has a nose quite like an elephant's! A trunk works like a nose, but it does so much more than just sniff at things. This is because it is more like an extra arm than a smelling organ. It is made up of the elephant's upper lip, nose and face muscles that have all joined together.

Elephants' trunks are packed with muscles, making them strong, bendy and very useful. They do not have any bones and that means they can move, stretch and curl in a way that limbs can't. A trunk is used for breathing and smelling, but it is also used for holding, grabbing, greeting and fighting.

◀ Elephant trunks developed over millions of years. Early ancestors used their smaller trunks like snorkels to breathe underwater.

African elephant

Asian elephant

▲ The trunk of an African elephant ends in two tips, whereas the trunk of the Asian has just one tip.

▼ The inside of an elephant's trunk is packed with powerful muscles that surround two tubes – the nostrils.

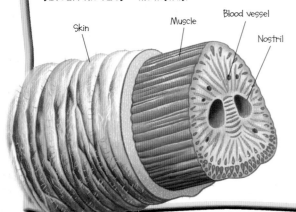

Skin

Muscle

Blood vessel

Nostril

The trunks of African and Asian elephants are slightly different. An African elephant's trunk has two tips that work like fingers that can hold small things, such as a flower or a seed. The trunk of an Asian elephant only has one tip, but it can still pick up small objects.

Without its trunk, an elephant would find it impossible to eat. Trunks pull food from the ground or bushes, but they also reach into trees for leaves and fruit that other animals can't reach. Elephants have been known to use their trunks to throw stones at people, too!

▶ Trunks stretch and move in many directions. As well as for eating, an elephant uses its trunk to wipe an eye, spray water and blow air on its skin.

An elephant pours water into its mouth with its trunk. Trunks work like straws, letting elephants suck up water. Once its trunk is full, the elephant lifts its head up and back, holds its trunk high above its mouth, and lets the water pour out.

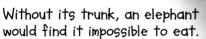

USE A TRUNK!

Make a mini-trunk using a drinking straw and a glass of water. Suck some water up a straw and place your finger over the top. What happens to the water? What happens if you release your finger? (Watch out!)

The trunk is so sensitive, an elephant can smell other animals that are far away. A male uses his sense of smell to find a female mate. A female also uses her trunk to stroke her calf (baby) when she is feeding it, to calm it if it is anxious.

◀ If they are too hot, elephants use their trunks to spray their bodies with cooling mud or water.

Teeth and tusks

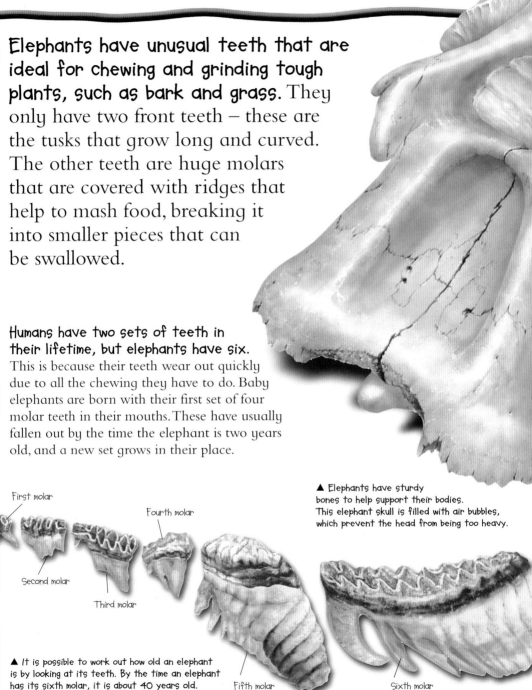

Elephants have unusual teeth that are ideal for chewing and grinding tough plants, such as bark and grass. They only have two front teeth – these are the tusks that grow long and curved. The other teeth are huge molars that are covered with ridges that help to mash food, breaking it into smaller pieces that can be swallowed.

Humans have two sets of teeth in their lifetime, but elephants have six. This is because their teeth wear out quickly due to all the chewing they have to do. Baby elephants are born with their first set of four molar teeth in their mouths. These have usually fallen out by the time the elephant is two years old, and a new set grows in their place.

First molar

Second molar

Third molar

Fourth molar

Fifth molar

Sixth molar

▲ Elephants have sturdy bones to help support their bodies. This elephant skull is filled with air bubbles, which prevent the head from being too heavy.

▲ It is possible to work out how old an elephant is by looking at its teeth. By the time an elephant has its sixth molar, it is about 40 years old.

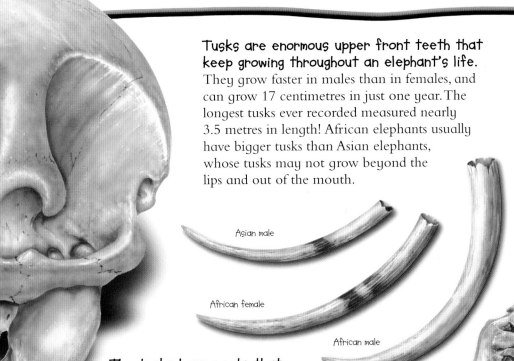

Tusks are enormous upper front teeth that keep growing throughout an elephant's life. They grow faster in males than in females, and can grow 17 centimetres in just one year. The longest tusks ever recorded measured nearly 3.5 metres in length! African elephants usually have bigger tusks than Asian elephants, whose tusks may not grow beyond the lips and out of the mouth.

Asian male

African female

African male

Mammoth

The tusks have roots that fit into the skull. The inside of the tooth contains blood, pulp and nerves. When tusks grow, they have enamel on them, but this soon wears away, leaving a creamy-white substance called ivory.

▲ The biggest tusks belonged to mammoths. Today, the African male elephant has the biggest tusks.

I DON'T BELIEVE IT!

Older elephants may die because the ridges on their teeth have worn away, causing the elephants to starve.

Tusks are not used as teeth, but as tools and weapons. They are used to dig in the dry soil for tasty roots to eat. Male elephants use their tusks to fight one another, and when elephants get tired, they often rest their heavy trunks on their tusks for a while!

Mighty meals

Elephants are herbivores, which means they only eat plants. However, plants are hard to digest (break down in the stomach and intestines). Getting goodness from plants is so difficult that herbivores spend most of their time eating and digesting food.

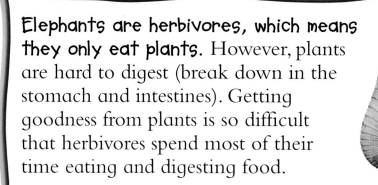

▼ Many trees that elephants like to eat are covered in spines. This elephant barely notices the prickly bits on this acacia bush.

Around two-thirds of an elephant's time is spent eating, and one elephant can get through 200 kilograms of food in a day. They eat grass, reeds, shrubs, leaves, branches, bark, flowers, fruits and seeds. Their trunks pull food from trees or the ground. They use their toenails and tusks to dig up tubers and roots.

QUIZ

Herbivores eat plants and carnivores eat meat. Do you know which of these animals are carnivores, and which are herbivores?

Tiger Hippo Owl
Dolphin

Answers:
Herbivore: hippo
Carnivores: tiger, owl, dolphin

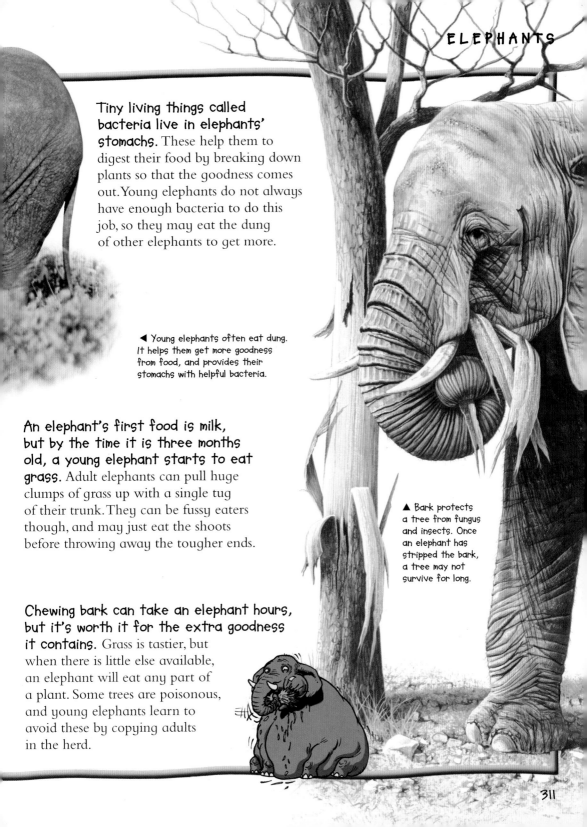

Tiny living things called bacteria live in elephants' stomachs. These help them to digest their food by breaking down plants so that the goodness comes out. Young elephants do not always have enough bacteria to do this job, so they may eat the dung of other elephants to get more.

◀ Young elephants often eat dung. It helps them get more goodness from food, and provides their stomachs with helpful bacteria.

An elephant's first food is milk, but by the time it is three months old, a young elephant starts to eat grass. Adult elephants can pull huge clumps of grass up with a single tug of their trunk. They can be fussy eaters though, and may just eat the shoots before throwing away the tougher ends.

▲ Bark protects a tree from fungus and insects. Once an elephant has stripped the bark, a tree may not survive for long.

Chewing bark can take an elephant hours, but it's worth it for the extra goodness it contains. Grass is tastier, but when there is little else available, an elephant will eat any part of a plant. Some trees are poisonous, and young elephants learn to avoid these by copying adults in the herd.

Fun at the waterhole

Elephants enjoy splashing in water, and a waterhole is a perfect place to cool down, drink, play and rest. Elephants live in hot places, and when they are feeling uncomfortable in the heat, they make their way to a waterhole or river to paddle, wallow and swim.

All elephants are excellent swimmers. They often dip below the water's surface using their trunks as snorkels to breathe. Some have even been seen to roll right over, so only the soles of their feet can be seen poking above the water!

Elephants are mammals. This means they have warm blood and give birth to live babies. Most mammals have fur to protect their skin from the sun and wind, but elephants have little body hair. This means that their skin can get dry and damaged. At a waterhole, elephants coat their skin in mud to cool and protect it.

▶ All elephants are usually grey in colour. They may appear to be brown or even reddish-brown if they have coated their skins in mud at a waterhole.

Elephants can use their ears like giant fans to cool down their whole bodies. The huge ears are full of blood vessels, and when an elephant flaps them, air moves all around, cooling the blood inside. The blood travels to other parts of the body, helping the elephant to control its temperature.

Female elephants

Elephants live in family groups that are led by the females. A group of elephants is called a herd and the leader is called a matriarch. She is normally the oldest female and is related to all the other females and youngsters in the herd. The matriarch can use her great age and experience to protect the herd, and lead it to food and water.

Female elephants start their own families when they are aged about ten, and they have calves every four to six years. They stop having calves when they are about 60, but by then they are grandmothers, or even great-grandmothers, and they help to look after all the young elephants in a herd.

▲ These two young elephants obey the older females in their herd. If they are in trouble, or scared, they rely on the matriarch to protect them.

▲ Females work together to keep the herd safe. When threatened, older family members form a circle around the youngsters. When they walk in file, the youngsters stay close to the adults, who keep watch for predators.

Calves are looked after by all females in the herd. Females as young as six start to care for younger brothers or sisters. This is good practice for motherhood. When they are teenagers, females are shown how to attract males by their mothers and grandmothers.

▲ This lion cub is at risk from female elephants, who know it may grow up to prey on elephant calves.

An African elephant called Nzou adopted a herd of buffaloes. She was an orphan elephant who grew up with buffaloes on a ranch. As she grew older, she became their leader and protected the females, but she started killing the males. The male buffaloes had to be moved and Nzou was left to rule her herd.

Female elephants can be aggressive. They may kill any lion cubs they come across on their travels. If an elephant sees lions near her calf, she will come running, trumpeting loudly to scare the lions away.

Bull elephants

Male elephants (bulls) leave their families when they are 10 to 15 years old. The females push them out of the herd, and never let them return. They spend their lives feeding, fighting and looking for females to mate with.

Young males join groups of other males, and start to learn how to be like them. Some live alone, but most try to tag along with a group of older males. They watch them as they fight for mates, and learn these important skills for themselves. They don't usually mate with females until they are about 25 years old.

▶ Adult male elephants are called bulls and they either live alone or in small groups of males. They are more unpredictable and aggressive than females.

I DON'T BELIEVE IT!

Elephants in musth may be aggressive. To prevent this, Asian elephants used to be given drugs, or less food. This stopped them going into musth.

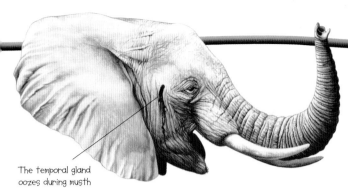

The temporal gland oozes during musth

▲ Males come into musth when they are about 25 years old.

When males are ready to mate, they are said to be in 'musth'. This is a dangerous time as the males become aggressive towards one another. Glands between their eyes and ears produce an oozing substance. This warns other elephants that they are in a fighting mood.

Males use their trunks and tusks to fight each another. They wrap their trunks together to test each other's strength, and push and pull. They use their tusks like swords, knocking and prodding each other. Serious injury is rare, as elephants back down when they know they have lost the fight.

All elephants continue to grow throughout their lives, and males grow more than females. The bigger males win more fights, and they are more successful in mating with females.

▲ Fighting bulls face each other, shaking their heads. The male with the bigger tusks is likely to win a fight, and get to mate with a female.

Big babies

◀ Baby elephants are called calves. When they are born they are unsteady on their feet and need their mothers to look after them all the time.

Elephants are mammals and feed their babies on milk, just like humans. Females have special glands that produce milk, which is a perfect first food for newborns. The newborn elephant gains up to 5 kilograms a day – that's the same weight as five bags of sugar!

Female elephants are pregnant for 22 months. During this time the baby elephant grows inside them. When the mother gives birth, females in her herd help her clean the baby and chase away any other curious animals. Within 30 minutes, the calf attempts to stand and stretch its legs.

▶ Newborn African elephants weigh more than most adult humans! Male calves can weigh as much as 120 kilograms.

▲ Baby elephants form close bonds with other youngsters in their herd. They often touch and smell one another.

Calves have short trunks, and they don't quite know what to do with them. Until they have practised using the muscles in their trunks, which can take several months, they are unable to control this extra limb. A calf can curl its trunk over its head when it feeds from its mother, but that's about all!

Newborns are welcomed into the herd by all the family members. They are allowed to come close and sniff the baby and touch it gently, introducing themselves. Before long, the youngster will be able to play with its cousins, brothers and sisters.

QUIZ

Elephants are mammals. Which of these animals are also mammals and feed their babies on milk?

Mouse Dolphin Lizard
Emu Cat Worm

Answer:
The mouse, dolphin and cat are mammals and feed their babies on milk.

Baby elephants continue to feed on their mother's milk until they are about four months old. During this time, the mother needs to eat and drink plenty of water and for this reason females usually give birth in the rainy season. The babies rely on their mothers for protection, food and affection for many years. If a mother elephant dies before her calf is two years old, it is unlikely the calf will survive.

Intelligent creatures

Elephants have big brains and are intelligent animals. Like humans, they are born fairly helpless and have a long 'childhood'. They need to learn how to communicate, how to live in a group, how to find food and water and how to stay safe from predators. This learning pays off, because some elephants live to the age of 70 years old.

These amazing animals are quick to learn new skills. Elephants that live close to humans may learn to copy some of the things we do, such as turning on taps or opening doors. If elephants look in a mirror, they recognize the image as themselves. Most animals think they are looking at another animal.

▲ Adult females stand over youngsters while they nap. They know which direction the sun is shining, and move so that their shadows always cover the sleeping babies.

◄ Zoo elephants can pick up a paintbrush and paint. Many seem to enjoy doing this!

Elephants can draw and doodle. In the wild, they may pick up sticks and doodle in the sand but no one knows why they do this, or whether they enjoy doing it. Elephants in zoos have been given paintbrushes and paper and have made pictures, some of which sell for large amounts of money.

In the same way as humans and other intelligent animals, Elephants use tools. Mothers teach their youngsters how to strip branches from a tree and use them to swat irritating flies away. They also use sticks to scratch their backs, and pick up objects to play with, or throw.

Farmers may use electric fences to protect their crops from elephants. However, these clever creatures have been known to pick up logs, carry them to the fence and drop them on it. Once the fence has been smashed, the elephant can walk over it without getting a shock, and eat the food.

▼ Cameras disguised as heaps of dung have been used to film elephants. Scientists watch the films to find out more about how these intelligent animals behave.

Communication

Elephants use different ways to communicate with one another, just like we do. We can talk, but we also use body language. This is the expressions on our faces and the way we hold or move our bodies, which gives other people information about the way we are feeling. Elephants also use their voices and body language to communicate.

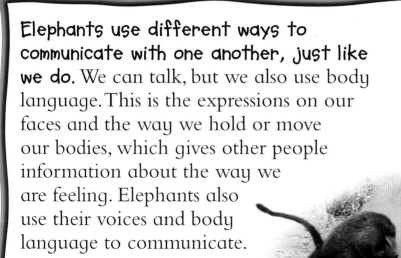

▶ When elephants show anger they use body language, such as flapping their ears and standing tall. These are signs to other animals, such as this baboon, that they should back away, quickly.

When they are excited, angry or scared, elephants make loud trumpeting calls. This is communication, and it works well when an elephant needs to let animals nearby know how it is feeling. Elephants make a trumpeting sound by blowing air through their trunks.

◀ A trumpeting elephant can be heard from up to 10 kilometres away.

I DON'T BELIEVE IT!

Zoo elephants need to keep their feet in good condition so they can 'listen' to vibrations. So keepers trim their nails and remove tough skin in an elephant pedicure!

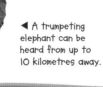

▶ An elephant's feet are cushioned by soft layers that pick up sounds. When walking, the feet spread out under the animal's weight.

Elephants listen to each another with their feet. When elephants rumble, the noise can travel through the ground for up to 10 kilometres. Other elephants detect these sounds as vibrations, which pass into their feet, through their skeletons and up to their ears.

Trunks also help elephants to communicate with each other. They put their trunks in one another's mouths to say hello, and they show each other how they are feeling by the position of their trunks. Mothers even use their trunks to smack their calves!

We are not able to hear some of what elephants say to each other because the sounds they make are too low. When elephants huddle together in a group they may often be 'talking' to each other, or to elephants far away. They do this by rumbling in a deep voice.

▶ Elephants may greet one another by wrapping their trunks together. They sniff each other and rumble a greeting.

Salt-lovers

A herd of elephants munches through tons of rock in some deep, dark caves. The rock contains salt, which the elephants need for their bodies to work properly. Animals that only eat plants, such as elephants, can't always get enough salt and other minerals in their normal diet. One way to get salt is to eat or lick rocks that contain it.

The caves shown here are inside a mountain called Mount Elgon, in Kenya, Africa. The elephants that live nearby regularly visit the caves. They dig out rock with their tusks and trunks to get to the salt and minerals.

Elephants' tongues are not long enough to lick salt, so they break off pieces of rock to eat. They use their tusks to do this, and over the years they can wear them down to stumps. They eat the rock using their huge molar teeth, which grind it down into smaller chunks to swallow. Elephants have eaten so much rock, it's possible that the caves have been entirely created by elephants 'mining' them.

The elephants pass through pitch-black tunnels to reach the salty walls. They use their trunks to feel their way as they travel deep into the mountainside. They walk in single file, taking care to avoid deep holes and cracks in the rocky cave floor.

▲ All elephants need salt in their diet. When adult elephants set off to the salt caves, the young elephants follow them. They learn how to dig for salt by copying the adults.

I SPY SALT

Salt is an important part of human diets, but too much of it can damage our health. Look on the sides of cereal packets, or other foods, to see how much salt one serving contains. Do some foods have much more salt than others?

The ivory trade

People have killed animals
for millions of years.
They are killed for meat
to eat, and for fur and
skins to provide warm
clothing. More recently,
animals are killed for
less important reasons.
Elephants have suffered
because people value
their white tusks, which
are made of ivory.

▶ During the Ice Age, food was scarce. People
laid traps and hunted in groups for mammoths.
These huge beasts provided food, fur and ivory.

Ivory is a very valuable substance that can be bought
and sold for large amounts of money. It was once used to
make items such as carved ornaments, jewellery, piano keys
and billiard balls. Before modern materials were invented,
such as plastic, people had fewer materials with
which to make things. Ivory was a popular
choice because it is smooth, creamy–white
and hard-wearing.

▲ A tusk can be carved with beautiful
designs as it does not break or chip
easily. Ivory ornaments are popular in
Japan and other Asian countries.

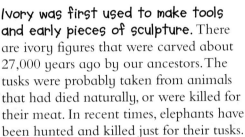

▼ Mammoth tusks were used to make carvings of other animals, such as this early sculpture of a cormorant, a type of bird.

Ivory was first used to make tools and early pieces of sculpture. There are ivory figures that were carved about 27,000 years ago by our ancestors. The tusks were probably taken from animals that had died naturally, or were killed for their meat. In recent times, elephants have been hunted and killed just for their tusks.

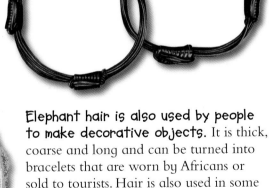

▶ Elephant hair bracelets are made with the tail hairs of elephants, which can reach one metre in length.

QUIZ

Ivory is a natural material. Which of these materials are natural, and which are man-made?

Wool Plastic Glass
Cotton Leather

Answer:
Wool, cotton and leather are natural, the others are man-made

Elephant hair is also used by people to make decorative objects. It is thick, coarse and long and can be turned into bracelets that are worn by Africans or sold to tourists. Hair is also used in some traditional medicines. The tough skin of an elephant can be treated, or cured, to become leather. Elephant leather is used to make shoes or fancy table tops.

At work and play

Thanks to their great intelligence and calm nature, elephants can be trained to help people work. They are used to lift and carry heavy objects, especially in places where vehicles and big machinery can't be used. Asian elephants have been logging for centuries – this involves moving huge logs that have been cut from trees in forests.

Elephants can be trained to carry people on their backs and take them through forests, or across grasslands, looking for other animals. These animal safaris are very popular with tourists as they provide jobs for elephant trainers, and help to protect the environment from pollution.

Elephants can be trained in different ways, some of which can be cruel. In the past, Asian elephant calves were taken from their mothers and chained to posts by their ankles. They were sometimes beaten until they learned to do what their trainers wanted.

▶ In Thailand, Asian elephants work at tourist sites, giving people rides. This gives local people jobs, and helps them to value their elephant neighbours.

Elephants in Thailand were banned from logging work in the 1980s, because too much of the precious forests had been cut down. The elephants were left without any work to do, until they were taken to the cities to help with building work.

African elephants help vets get close to dangerous beasts, such as rhinos. When rhinos are ill and need medical help they can become dangerous. If a vet approaches on an elephant's back, the rhino remains calm and can be shot with a tranquilising dart. The dart sends the rhino to sleep while the vet takes care of it.

WORK THAT NOSE!

How easy would you find it to pick up a pencil using your nose and your upper lip? Would you be able to roll it along the floor with your nose? Try it and see!

Elephants don't just work, they get to play, too! In India and Nepal, elephants take part in a game called polo. Riders on their backs have long sticks that they use to hit balls across a pitch. The elephants are treated to drinks and nibbles at half time, and a dip in the river every day!

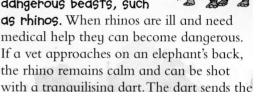

Keystone creatures

▼ Vultures are birds that feed on dead or rotting meat. When an elephant dies, its body is eaten by animals and birds, helping them to live and breed.

Without elephants, other animals and plants would die. For this reason they are called keystone creatures. Elephants help to shape the habitat (place they live), and this has an effect on other forms of life.

As they stroll through forests or grasslands, elephants drop lots of dung. The dung is full of coarse plant fibres that their bodies have not been able to digest. Seeds in the dung can begin to grow into new plants. In this way, elephants help to spread plants to new areas.

◄ This baboon finds a meal by picking out seeds and undigested plant matter from elephant dung.

Some beetles gather elephant dung and roll it into a ball. They lay their eggs in it and when the larvae (insect young) hatch, they eat it. Many other insects use dung as food, and without elephants they would be much rarer.

◄ Elephant dung, or manure, is like fertilizer for the soil. It contains many nutrients that animals, such as these dung beetles, and plants need to survive.

Elephants can damage farmers' crops as they search for food. Farmers often turn elephant feeding areas into fields, and the elephants do not understand that the new crops are not for them. If farmers plant rows of hot chilli bushes around their farms, the elephants stay away.

When a waterhole or river has dried up, elephants can dig to find water. They use their feet, trunks and tusks to remove soil until the water springs up. It is not only elephants who benefit from the water, but all the other animals nearby.

▼ Elephants trample plants and bushes as they walk. The dead plants provide food for fungi, insects, worms and other forms of life that are, in turn, eaten by birds, lizards and mammals.

Elephants can destroy plants as they march through vegetation on the way to find food or water. For this reason many people think elephants do more harm to their habitat than good. But these pathways are useful for humans and other animals that need to get through dense forests. Elephants eventually change their routes, and the plants grow back.

I DON'T BELIEVE IT!

Egrets are birds that like to hop about on the back of an elephant. They get a free ride, and can munch bugs and flies that dart around the elephant's feet.

Circle of life

All animals must die to make room on the planet for the next generation. Elephants live longer than most animals, but not all of them die of old age or disease. Like all wild creatures, they face dangers and difficulties – and survival can be a battle against the odds.

Humans have been taking the lives of elephants for hundreds of years. Now many populations of elephants are in danger of dying out completely. In the past, elephants were shot for sport and for their ivory. Nowadays they are more likely to lose their lives in the battle for space. In parts of Asia, especially, elephants are shot or electrocuted to keep them off farmland. They also get injured on roads and railways, or walk on unexploded landmines.

▼ No one knows how many elephants have been killed for their ivory. When ivory is found, it is taken by the government and destroyed so it can never be sold.

▲ Elephants sometimes visit the remains of a dead family member, touching the bones gently with their trunks.

It is possible to find the skeletons of several elephants near waterholes. This led to the belief in elephant graveyards, where elephants went to die. It's more likely that when some elephants are dying, they make their way to water, which they hope will make them better.

Elephants are known to grieve when a member of their family dies. When an elephant is dying, others try to help it get up. When it dies, members of the family stand around the body. They return to visit the body days later, and touch it gently with their trunks.

▶ Mothers have been known to stand by the bodies of their dead calves for up to three days.

Tomorrow's world

Elephants may not survive into the next century. The human population is growing in areas where elephants live, and their habitats are being turned into farms. In some places there is little food for people and they kill elephants for meat, or their tusks.

Elephant orphanages have been set up in Africa and Asia to look after young elephants. Some of the animals have lost their mothers to poachers. Animal experts rescue them, with the hope that one day they can start new herds and go back to the wild.

Groups of people called conservationists work hard to save elephants. They study elephants to gain a better understanding of how they live. Conservationists hope to find new ways that humans and elephants can live side by side.

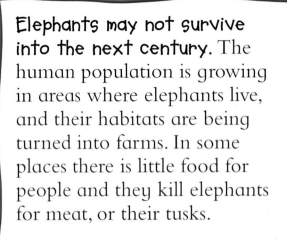

▼ These young Asian elephants are in an orphanage. Here they are fed and protected from poachers.

▲ Tourists flock to African safari parks, where they can watch animals, including elephants, in their natural surroundings.

▲ This elephant is wearing a radio transmitter. It allows scientists to study how the elephant behaves and where it travels.

Tourism can bring elephants and people together in a positive way. Thousands of tourists visit countries with elephants every year, bringing money and work for local people. Seeing elephants up close helps people to understand these majestic, beautiful beasts.

Scientists study elephants in the wild.
They work in reserves, which are special areas that are protected from farmers and poachers. Elephants are fitted with radio transmitters, so scientists can follow their movements over many years.

Teaching people to value elephants is a big step towards protecting them for the future.
Schools in Africa and Asia teach children about elephants, and how important they are to the environment. Farmers are taught new ways to protect their crops, without harming hungry elephants.

Deadly Creatures

Discover some of the fiercest and most dangerous creatures on Earth, from man-eating sharks to venomous snakes.

Claws and teeth • Big cats • Wolves
Crocodiles and alligators • Birds of prey
Piranhas • Venom • Spiders • Defences
Sharks • Insects

A fight to survive

The world is full of animals that are fighting to survive. There are many reasons why animals may attack one another. Some are called predators and they kill for food. Others only kill to defend themselves, their young or their homes. Whatever the reason for using their claws, jaws, poisons or stings, these creatures are fascinating, but deadly.

▼ To catch its prey, the Nile crocodile lies very still in the water until the gazelle comes close. Then it shoots out of its hiding place, trying to catch the gazelle in its powerful jaws.

Killer carnivores

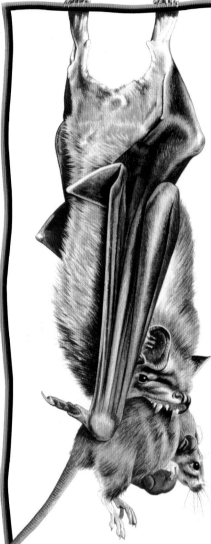

◀ False vampire bats have very sharp teeth, like the vampire bat. They catch and feed on frogs, mice, birds and other bats.

Animals that eat meat are called carnivores. Scavengers are carnivores that steal meat from others, or find dead animals to eat. Most carnivores, however, have to hunt and kill. These animals are called predators.

Killer whales are some of the largest predators in the world. Despite their size, these mighty beasts often hunt in groups called pods. By working together, killer whales can kill large animals, including other whales. However, they usually hunt smaller creatures, such as sea lions and dolphins.

▼ Anacondas are types of boa, and are the heaviest snakes in the world. As they don't have chewing teeth, snakes swallow their prey whole. Anacondas feed on large rodents called capybara, deer, fish and birds.

Vampire bats do not eat meat, but they do feed on other animals. With their razor-sharp teeth, vampire bats pierce the skin of a sleeping animal, such as a horse or pig, and drink their blood. False vampire bats are bigger, and they eat the flesh of other animals.

With their cold eyes and gaping mouths, piranhas are fierce-looking predators. When a shoal, or group, of piranhas attack, they work together like an enormous slicing machine. Within minutes, they can strip a horse to its skeleton using their tiny triangular teeth.

▲ Red piranhas are aggressive, speedy predators. They work together in a group to attack their prey, such as birds.

Some snakes rely on venom, or poison, to kill their prey, but constrictors squeeze their victims to death. Pythons and boas wrap their enormous bodies around the victim. Every time the captured animal breathes out, the snake squeezes a little tighter, until its prey can no longer breathe.

341

Lethal weapons

Many animals have deadly weapons, including teeth, claws, horns and stings. They are perfect for killing prey, or fighting enemies.

Inside the mouth of a meat-eating predator is an impressive collection of deadly daggers – teeth. Different teeth do different jobs. Canines, or fangs, are long and knife-like, and are used to grab prey or pierce skin. Teeth at the front of the mouth are very sharp, and are ideal for cutting and slicing flesh.

◄ Mandrills are part of the same family as monkeys, called primates. Males bare their enormous fangs when they are anxious, or want to scare other males. The fangs may reach up to 7 centimetres in length.

Stings are common weapons in the animal world and they are used by creatures – such as jellyfish and scorpions. Stings usually contain poison, or venom. The stingray, for example, is a fish with a long saw-shaped spine on its tail, which is coated in poison.

Elephant and walrus tusks are overgrown teeth that make fearsome weapons when used to stab and lunge at attackers. Males use their tusks to fight one another at mating time, or to scare away predators. An elephant can kill a person with a single thrust from its mighty tusks.

FIND YOUR FANGS

You have cutting and chewing teeth, too. Use a mirror to find them.

Incisors are the sharp, flat teeth at the front of your mouth. They are used for cutting and tearing food.

Canines are the pointy teeth next to the incisors, used for piercing food.

Molars are at the back of your mouth. They are used for grinding food.

▼ Birds of prey grab hold of their victim with powerful talons, which pierce the flesh with ease.

▼ Cats have sharp claws that can be pulled back into the paws when they are not being used.

Some animals fight for mates, or territory (the area they live in). Horned animals, such as deer, are not predators, but they may fight and attack other animals. These animals have been known to harm humans when they are scared.

Eagles have huge claws called talons. The bird grasps prey in its feet, killing it by piercing and squeezing with its talons. Eagles and other carnivorous (meat-eating) birds are called birds of prey.

▲ Ibex are wild goats. They use their thick, curved horns to fight for mates or territory. Horns can be used to stab, wound and even kill.

Silent hunters

Agile and fast, with sharp teeth and claws, cats are some of the deadliest predators in the world. Most cats hunt alone, but lions works as a team to catch their prey.

In Asia, many people are fearful of living near tigers. However, tigers hunt small creatures, such as birds, monkeys and reptiles. They have been known to attack bigger animals, such as rhinos and elephants, but it is rare for them to kill humans.

A group of lions is called a pride, and the females are the hunters. Cubs spend hours play-fighting. This helps them to practise the skills they will need to catch and kill prey when they are older.

▼ Lionesses hunt in a group, which means they can attack big, aggressive animals, such as buffaloes.

Cheetahs are the fastest hunters on land, and can reach speeds of more than 100 kilometres an hour. Despite their great speed, cheetahs often fail to catch the animal they are chasing. Although these cats have great spurts of energy, they tire very quickly. If cheetahs have not caught their prey in about 30 seconds, it may escape – this time.

Leopards are secretive killers. They live throughout Africa and Asia, but are rarely seen. They are agile climbers and spend much of their time in trees, waiting for unsuspecting animals to wander by. Like most cats, leopards kill prey by sinking their huge teeth into the victim's neck.

Big, bold and beastly

Big, white and fluffy, polar bears look cuddly, but they are deadly predators. Occasionally, polar bears travel from the icy Arctic to small towns in search of food. At these times, they are hungry and dangerous, and may attack.

Polar bears use their huge paws to swim with ease underwater. They can hold their breath for several minutes, waiting until the time is right to swim up and grab their prey. On land, these ferocious bears hunt by creeping up on their prey, then pouncing, leaving the victim with no escape.

▼ A polar bear's paw is as big as a dinner plate, and is equipped with five big claws, one on each toe.

◄ Polar bears are meat-eaters. They wait by a seal's breathing hole for the seal to appear above the water. With one swift bite, the bear kills its prey and drags it out of the water.

QUIZ

1. Which bear would you find in the Arctic?
2. Which fairytale character ate the three bears' porridge?
3. Which slippery creatures do brown bears like to eat?

Answers:
1. Polar bear 2. Goldilocks 3. Salmon

Grizzlies are brown bears of North America. They often come into contact with humans when searching for food and raiding rubbish bins, and are considered to be extremely dangerous. Grizzlies often live in woods and forests. They mainly feed on berries, fruit, bulbs and roots, but also fish for salmon in fast-flowing rivers.

▲ Kodiak bears live in Alaska where they eat fish, grass, plants and berries. They only bare their teeth and roar to defend themselves against predators.

Black bears in Asia rarely attack humans, but when they do, the attack is often fatal. Asian black bears are herbivores. This means that they eat plants rather than meat. If they are scared, these shy animals may attack to kill.

Brown bears are one of the largest meat eaters in the world, and can stand more than 3 metres tall. They are powerful animals, with long front claws and strong jaws.

▶ Brown bears catch salmon as they leap out of the water. A snap of the jaws is enough to grab the wriggling fish.

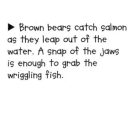

Skills to kill

Monkeys and apes belong to the same group of animals as humans, called primates. These intelligent creatures have great skills of communication and teamwork. Although monkeys, gorillas and chimps appear to be playful, they can be dangerous.

It was once believed that chimps only ate plants and insects. However, it has been discovered that groups of chimps ambush and attack colobus monkeys. Each chimp takes its own role in the hunting team. During the chase, the chimps communicate with each other by screeching and hooting.

Chimps also kill each other. Groups of male chimps patrol the forest, looking for males from another area. If they find one, the group may gang up on the stranger and kill him.

▶ Chimps use their great intelligence to organize hunts. Some of them scream, hoot and chase the colobus monkey. Other chimps in the group hide, ready to attack.

Baboons live in family groups and eat a wide range of foods, from seeds to antelopes. Young males eventually leave their family, and fight with other males to join a new group and find mates.

A mighty gorilla may seem fierce, but it is actually one of the most gentle primates. Large adult males, called silverbacks, only charge to protect their families by scaring other animals, or humans, away. Gorillas can inflict terrible bite wounds with their fearsome fangs.

I DON'T BELIEVE IT!

Chimps are skilled at making and using tools. It is easy for them to hold sticks and rocks in their hands. They use sticks to break open insects' nests and they use rocks to smash nuts.

349

Canine killers

Wolves, coyotes and African hunting dogs belong to the dog family. Most live and hunt in groups, or packs. By working together, a pack can attack and kill large prey, such as deer and bison.

◄ When a wolf feels threatened, the fur on its back, called its hackles, stands on end. This makes it look bigger and fiercer.

Wolves have excellent senses of sight, hearing and smell to help them to find their prey. These strong, agile creatures have been known to travel a distance of 100 kilometres in just one night in search of food.

Coyotes are wild dogs that live in North America. They normally hunt in pairs or on their own, although they may join together as a group to chase large prey, such as deer.

Like wild cats, coyotes hunt by keeping still and watching an animal nearby. They wait for the right moment, then creep towards their prey and pounce, landing on top of the startled victim. Coyotes are swift runners and often chase jackrabbits across rocks and up hills.

▶ When African hunting dogs pursue their prey, such as the wildebeest, the chase may go on for several kilometres, but the dogs rarely give up. They wait until their prey tires, then leap in for the kill.

BE A WOLF!

1. One person is Mr Wolf and stands with their back to the other players.
2. The players stand 10 paces away and shout, "What's the time, Mr Wolf?".
3. If Mr Wolf shouts, "It's 10 o'clock", the players take 10 steps towards Mr Wolf.
4. Watch out because when Mr Wolf shouts "Dinnertime", he chases the other players and whoever he catches is out of the game!

African wild dogs are deadly pack hunters. They work as a team to chase and torment their prey. The whole pack shares the meal, tearing at the meat with their sharp teeth.

Ambush and attack

Lurking beneath the surface of the water, a deadly hunter waits, ready to pounce. Lying absolutely still, only its eyes and nostrils are visible. With one swift movement, the victim is dragged underwater. This killer is the crocodile, a relative of the dinosaurs.

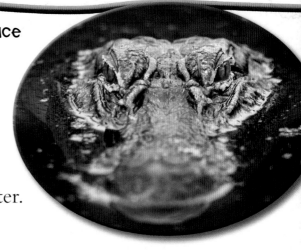

▲ Crocodiles and alligators are well-suited to their aquatic lifestyle. They spend much of their day in water, keeping cool and hidden from view.

Only teeth in the upper jaw are visible

Alligator

▲▼ When a crocodile's mouth is closed, some of the teeth on its lower jaw can be seen. Alligators have wide u-shaped jaws, but the jaws of crocodiles are narrow and v-shaped.

Teeth in the lower jaw can be seen

Crocodile

When a crocodile has its prey in sight, it moves at lightning speed. The prey has little chance to escape as the crocodile pulls it underwater. Gripping the victim in its mighty jaws, the crocodile twists and turns in a 'deathspin' until its victim has drowned.

The largest crocodiles in the world live in estuaries, where rivers meet the oceans. They are called estuarine crocodiles and can reach a staggering 7 metres in length. These giant predators are often known as man-eating crocodiles, although they are most likely to catch turtles, snakes, monkeys, cows and pigs.

Alligators are very strong reptiles with wide jaws and thick, scaly skin on their backs. They live in marshes, ponds and rivers, often close to where people live. Like all crocodiles and alligators, the American alligator will catch and eat anything. They have even been known to attack humans.

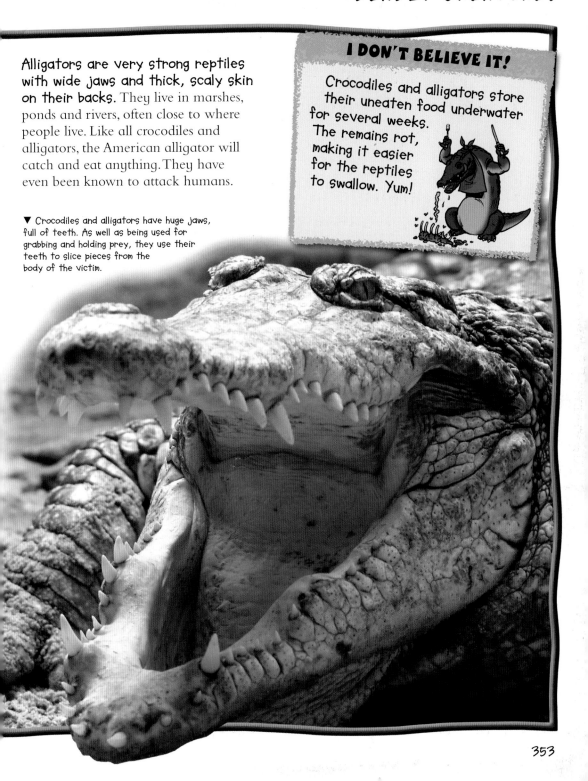

▼ Crocodiles and alligators have huge jaws, full of teeth. As well as being used for grabbing and holding prey, they use their teeth to slice pieces from the body of the victim.

I DON'T BELIEVE IT!

Crocodiles and alligators store their uneaten food underwater for several weeks. The remains rot, making it easier for the reptiles to swallow. Yum!

Ravenous raptors

Eagles, hawks, kites and ospreys are fearsome predators called birds of prey. Equipped with incredible eyesight, powerful legs, and sharp claws and bills, they hunt during the day, soaring high in the sky as they look for food.

▶ Eagle owls are large, powerful birds. They hunt and capture large animals, including other owls and birds of prey.

Birds do not have teeth. They have bills, or beaks, instead. Tearing large pieces of meat is a difficult job using just a bill. Birds of prey use their curved claws, called talons, to hold or rip their food apart, or they just swallow it whole.

Birds of prey are also known as raptors, which comes from the Latin word 'rapere', meaning 'to seize'. Once they have captured their prey, such as a mouse, bird or frog, a raptor usually takes it to its nest to start pulling off fur and feathers. Bones are also thrown away, and the ground near a raptor's nest may be strewn with animal remains.

▶ Like most birds of prey, golden eagles have razor-sharp, hooked bills. They use them to tear the body of their prey apart.

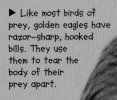

Little more than the flap of a wing can be heard as an owl swoops down to grab an unsuspecting mouse. Owls hunt at night. They can even see small movements on the ground, thanks to their large eyes and sharp eyesight. When they hunt in total darkness, they rely on their excellent sense of hearing to find food.

The names of raptors
have been jumbled up. Can
you work out what they are?

1. GELEA   4. LOW
2. ITKE   5. PRYESO
3. CFALNO   6. KAWH

Answers:
1. Eagle 2. Kite 3. Falcon
4. Owl 5. Osprey 6. Hawk

Peregrine falcons are the fastest hunters in the world, reaching speeds of up to 230 kilometres an hour as they swoop down to attack other birds. Peregrines hunt on the wing. This means that they catch their prey while in flight. They chase their prey to tire it out, before lashing out with their sharp talons.

▼ Bald eagles live on a diet of fish, which they swipe out of the water using their talons.

Ospreys dive, feet-first, into the water from a great height in pursuit of their prey. Fish may be slippery, but ospreys have spiky scales on the underside of the feet so they can grip more easily. Once ospreys have a fish firmly in their grasp, they fly away to find a safe place to eat.

Mighty monsters

Not all deadly creatures kill for food. Many of them only attack when they are frightened. Some plant-eating animals fight to protect their young, or when they feel scared.

African buffaloes can be very aggressive towards other animals and humans. If they become scared, they move quickly and attack with their huge horns. Groups of buffaloes surround a calf or ill member of the herd to protect it. They face outwards to prevent predators getting too close.

Hippos may appear calm when they are wallowing at the edge of a waterhole, but they kill more people in Africa than any other large animal. These huge creatures fiercely protect their own stretch of water, and females are extremely aggressive when they have calves and feel threatened.

If an elephant starts flapping its ears and trumpeting, it is giving a warning sign to stay away. However, when an elephant folds its ears back, curls its trunk under its mouth and begins to run – then it really means business. Elephants will attack to keep other animals or humans away from the infants in their herd, and males will fight one another for a mate.

With huge bodies and massive horns, rhinos look like fearsome predators. They are actually related to horses and eat a diet of leaves, grass and fruit. Rhinos can become aggressive, however, when they are scared. They have poor eyesight, which may be why they can easily feel confused or threatened, and attack without warning.

◄ Male hippos fight one another using their massive teeth as weapons. Severe injuries can occur, leading to the death of at least one of the hippos.

I DON'T BELIEVE IT!

Adult male elephants are called bulls, and they can become killers. A single stab from an elephant's tusk is enough to cause a fatal wound, and one elephant is strong enough to flip a car over onto its side!

Toxic tools

▶ Marine toads are the largest toads in the world. When they are threatened, venom oozes from the glands in the toad's skin. This poison could kill a small animal in minutes.

Some animals rely on teeth and claws to kill prey, but others have an even deadlier weapon called venom. Venom is the name given to any poison that is made by an animal's body. There are lots of different types of venom. Some cause only a painful sting, but others can result in death.

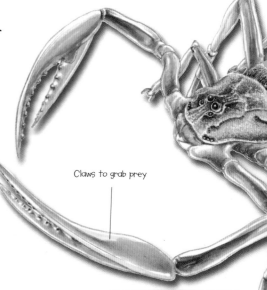

▼ The death stalker scorpion is one of the most dangerous scorpions in the world. It lives in North Africa and the Middle East. One sting can cause paralysis (loss of movement) and heart failure in humans.

Claws to grab prey

The marine toad produces venom from special areas, called glands, behind its eyes. The venom is not used to kill prey, but to protect the toad from being eaten by other animals because it is extremely poisonous if swallowed.

Many snakes have venom glands in their mouths. They use their fangs to inject poison straight into their victim's body. Venom is made from saliva mixed with deadly substances. Spitting cobras shoot venom from their mouths. This venom can cause blindness in humans.

Scorpions belong to the same group as spiders – arachnids. Instead of producing venom in their fangs, they have stings in their tails. They use venom to kill prey, such as lizards and mice, or to defend themselves. Few scorpions can cause serious injury to humans, but some, such as the death stalker scorpion, are deadly.

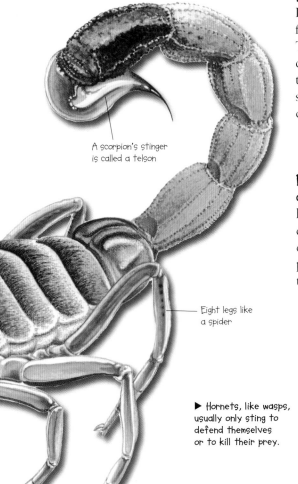

A scorpion's stinger is called a telson

Eight legs like a spider

Even small insects can harm other animals. Hornets, wasps and bees have stings in their tails that are attached to venom sacs. A single sting causes swelling and pain, and may prove fatal to people who are allergic to the venom.

▶ Hornets, like wasps, usually only sting to defend themselves or to kill their prey.

Sting

Scary snakes

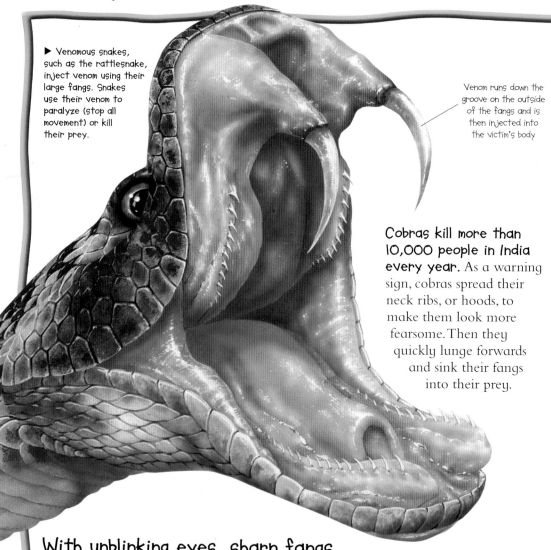

▶ Venomous snakes, such as the rattlesnake, inject venom using their large fangs. Snakes use their venom to paralyze (stop all movement) or kill their prey.

Venom runs down the groove on the outside of the fangs and is then injected into the victim's body

Cobras kill more than 10,000 people in India every year. As a warning sign, cobras spread their neck ribs, or hoods, to make them look more fearsome. Then they quickly lunge forwards and sink their fangs into their prey.

With unblinking eyes, sharp fangs and flickering tongues, snakes look like menacing killers. Despite their fearsome reputation, snakes only attack people when they feel threatened.

The taipan is one of Australia's most venomous snakes. When this snake attacks, it injects large amounts of venom that can kill a person in less than an hour.

Carpet vipers are small snakes found throughout many parts of Africa and Asia. They are responsible for hundreds, maybe thousands, of human deaths every year. Carpet viper venom affects the nervous system and the blood, causing the victim to bleed to death.

I DON'T BELIEVE IT!

Snakes can open their jaws so wide that they can swallow their prey whole. Large snakes, such as constrictors, can even swallow antelopes or pigs!

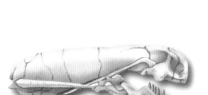

Short jaw that cannot open very wide

◀ Primitive snakes have a heavy skull with a short lower jaw and few teeth.

Gaboon vipers have the longest fangs of any snake, reaching 5 centimetres in length. They produce large amounts of venom, which they inject deeply into the flesh with dagger-like teeth. Although slow and calm by nature, Gaboon vipers attack with great speed and a single bite can kill a human in less than two hours.

Fangs are towards the rear of the mouth, below the eye

◀ Rear-fanged snakes have fangs in the roof of their mouths.

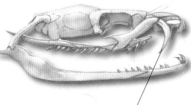

◀ Some snakes have fangs at the front of their mouths.

The fangs are hollow, and positioned at the front of the mouth

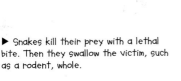
▶ Snakes kill their prey with a lethal bite. Then they swallow the victim, such as a rodent, whole.

Dragons and monsters

▼ Komodo dragons use their powerful jaws to tear the flesh of their victim, and then eat everything, including bones and fur.

Komodo dragons are not really dragons, but lizards. They can reach 3 metres in length and up to 100 kilograms in weight, making them the largest lizards in the world. They hunt their prey using their sensitive sense of smell.

Once the Komodo has caught its prey, it sinks its sharp teeth into the victim's flesh. With a mouth full of poisonous bacteria, one bite is enough to kill an animal with an infection, even if it escapes the Komodo's clutches.

QUIZ

1. What colour is the Gila monster?
2. Why does the fire salamander have bold patterns on its skin?
3. How does the Komodo dragon hunt its prey?

Answers:
1. Black, pink and yellow
2. To warn predators that it is poisonous 3. Using its sensitive sense of smell

There are only two truly poisonous lizards — the Gila monster and the Mexican beaded lizard. Gila monsters live in North America and they have bands of black, pink and yellow on their scaly skin to warn predators to stay away.

▶ Gila monsters use their sense of smell to hunt small animals and find reptile eggs. They can kill their prey with a single bite.

▼ Fire salamanders are amphibians, like frogs. They hunt insects and earthworms, mainly at night.

Fire salamanders look like a cross between a lizard and a frog. They have bold patterns on their skin to warn predators that they are poisonous. The poison, or toxin, is on their skin and tastes foul. They squirt the toxin at predators, irritating or even killing them.

363

Fearsome frogs

At first glance, few frogs appear fearsome. They may not have teeth or claws, but frogs and toads produce a deadly substance in their moist skin. This substance may taste foul or even be poisonous. The most poisonous frogs live in the forests of Central and South America. They are called poison-dart frogs.

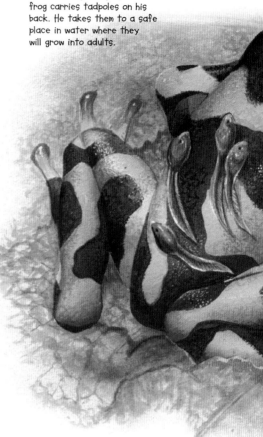

▶ The male green poison-dart frog carries tadpoles on his back. He takes them to a safe place in water where they will grow into adults.

One of the deadliest frogs is the golden poison-dart frog. It lives in rainforests in western Colombia, and its skin produces a very powerful poison – one of the deadliest known substances. A single touch is enough to cause almost instant death.

▼ The strawberry poison-dart frog is also known as the 'blue jeans' frog because of its blue legs.

Many poison-dart frogs are becoming rare in the wild. This is because the rainforests where they live are being cut down. Some poison-dart frogs can be kept in captivity, where they gradually become less poisonous. When they are raised in captivity, these frogs are not poisonous at all.

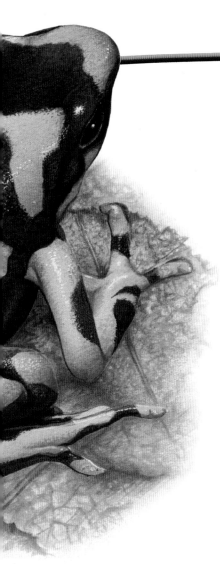

People who live in the rainforests of Central and South America use the poison from frogs to catch food. A hunter wipes the tip of a dart on the poisonous frog's back, then carefully puts it in a blowpipe. One puff sends the lethal dart into the body of an unsuspecting monkey or bird.

▼ Poison is wiped off the back of the golden poison-dart frog with a dart. One frog produces enough poison for more than 50 darts.

Looking after eggs is the job of male green poison-dart frogs. The female lays her eggs amongst the leaf litter on the forest floor. The male guards them until they hatch into tadpoles, then carries them to water, where they will grow into frogs.

365

Eight-legged hunters

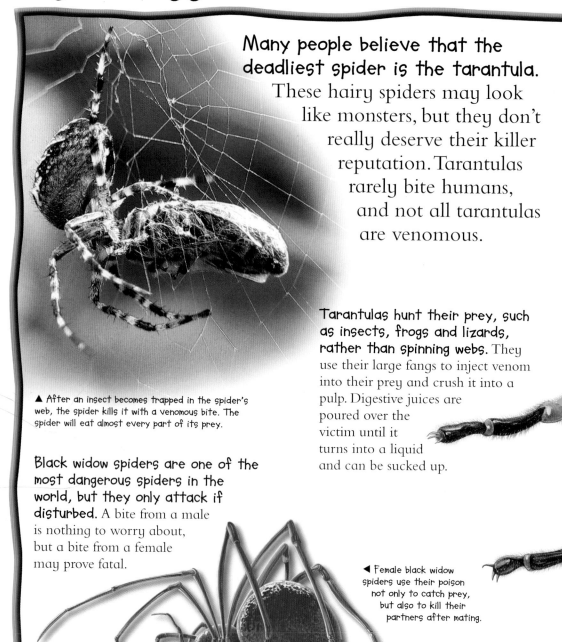

Many people believe that the deadliest spider is the tarantula. These hairy spiders may look like monsters, but they don't really deserve their killer reputation. Tarantulas rarely bite humans, and not all tarantulas are venomous.

▲ After an insect becomes trapped in the spider's web, the spider kills it with a venomous bite. The spider will eat almost every part of its prey.

Tarantulas hunt their prey, such as insects, frogs and lizards, rather than spinning webs. They use their large fangs to inject venom into their prey and crush it into a pulp. Digestive juices are poured over the victim until it turns into a liquid and can be sucked up.

Black widow spiders are one of the most dangerous spiders in the world, but they only attack if disturbed. A bite from a male is nothing to worry about, but a bite from a female may prove fatal.

◀ Female black widow spiders use their poison not only to catch prey, but also to kill their partners after mating.

Spiders belong to a group of animals called arachnids, along with scorpions and ticks. Some ticks can kill without using deadly poison. They attach themselves to the bodies of humans and other animals, and suck their blood. This can spread deadly diseases.

QUIZ

1. How do ticks kill animals?
2. Is the male or female black widow spider more dangerous?
3. Which spider stands on its hind legs when it feels threatened?

Answers:
1. They suck their blood and spread diseases 2. Female 3. Funnel web spider

There are many types of funnel web spider, and some of them are very venomous. When a funnel web spider is threatened, it stands on its hind legs and rears, showing its huge fangs. These killers bite their prey many times, injecting poison.

▲ The fangs of the funnel web spider are so strong that they can pierce human skin, even fingernails. Its bite can cause death in just 15 minutes.

367

Clever defenders

To survive in a dangerous world, animals need to be able to hide, fight or appear deadly. When it is threatened, the spiny puffer fish swallows large amounts of water, making its body swell up and its spines stand on end.

Spines can be used to pass venom into the victim's body, or used as weapons of defence. The long, sharp spines on the Cape porcupine are called quills, and they stick into an attacker's body, causing painful injuries.

▼▶ The spiny puffer fish stiffens and swells its body, changing from an ordinary-looking fish to a spiky ball.

◄ Tortoises are protected from predators by their tough shell. Even the sharp claws and teeth of lion cubs cannot break it.

Some animals hide from their predators using camouflage. This means the colour or pattern of an animal's skin blends in with its surroundings. Lizards called chameleons are masters of camouflage. They can change their skin colour from brown to green so they blend in with their background. They do this to communicate with one another.

The bold colours and pattern on the coral snake's skin warns predators that it is poisonous. The milk snake looks almost identical to the coral snake, but it is not venomous. Its colour keeps it safe though, because predators think it is poisonous.

I DON'T BELIEVE IT!

Electric eels have an unusual way of staying safe – they zap prey and predators with electricity! They can produce 600 volts of power at a time, which is enough to kill a human!

▶ The harmless milk snake looks similar to the venomous coral snake, so predators stay away. This life-saving animal trick is called mimicry.

Danger at sea

Deep in the ocean lurk some of the deadliest creatures in the world. There are keen-eyed killers, venomous stingers and sharp-toothed hunters, but as few of these animals come into contact with humans, attacks are rare.

▶ The Australian box jellyfish is also known as the sea wasp. Its tentacles can grow more than 3 metres in length and one animal has enough venom to kill 60 people.

Barracudas are long, strong, powerful fish. They lunge at their prey, baring dagger-like teeth. Although they prey on other fish, barracudas may mistake swimmers for food and attack them.

The box jellyfish is one of the most lethal creatures in the world. A touch from only one tentacle can kill a human. The floating body of a jellyfish is harmless, but danger lies in the many tentacles that drift below. Each tentacle is covered with tiny stingers that shoot venom into the victim.

◀ Barracudas are fierce fish with powerful jaws and sharp teeth.

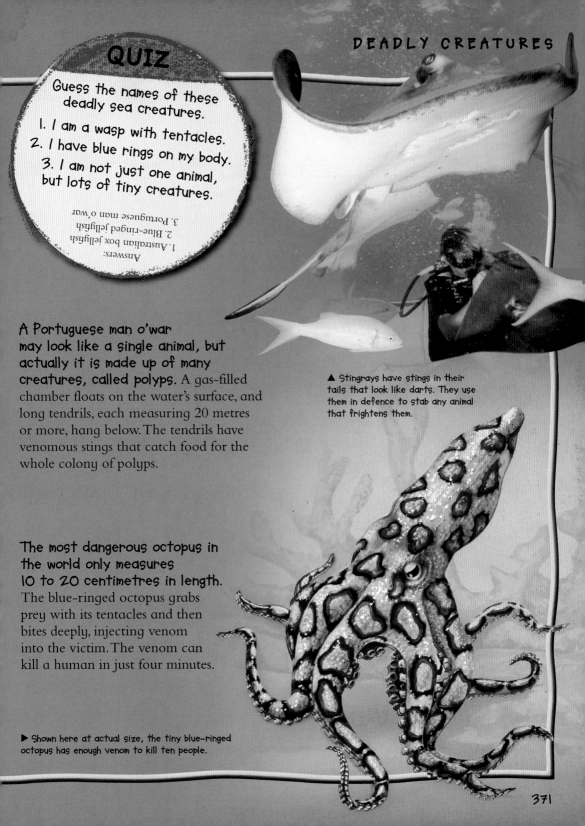

QUIZ

Guess the names of these deadly sea creatures.

1. I am a wasp with tentacles.
2. I have blue rings on my body.
3. I am not just one animal, but lots of tiny creatures.

Answers:
1. Australian box jellyfish
2. Blue-ringed jellyfish
3. Portuguese man o'war

A Portuguese man o'war may look like a single animal, but actually it is made up of many creatures, called polyps. A gas-filled chamber floats on the water's surface, and long tendrils, each measuring 20 metres or more, hang below. The tendrils have venomous stings that catch food for the whole colony of polyps.

▲ Stingrays have stings in their tails that look like darts. They use them in defence to stab any animal that frightens them.

The most dangerous octopus in the world only measures 10 to 20 centimetres in length. The blue-ringed octopus grabs prey with its tentacles and then bites deeply, injecting venom into the victim. The venom can kill a human in just four minutes.

▶ Shown here at actual size, the tiny blue-ringed octopus has enough venom to kill ten people.

371

Sharks in the shadows

Few animals send a shiver down the spine quite like a great white shark. This huge fish is a skilled hunter. Its bullet-shaped body can slice through the water at lightning speed, powered by huge muscles and a crescent-shaped tail.

Sharks are fish, and belong to the same family as rays and skates. Most sharks are predators and feed on fish, squid, seals and other sea creatures. Some sharks hunt with quick spurts of energy as they chase their prey. Others lie in wait for victims to pass by.

Bull sharks are a deadly threat to humans. This is because they live in areas close to human homes. They often swim inland, using the same rivers that people use to bathe and collect water, and may attack.

One of the deadliest sharks can be found in oceans and seas throughout the world. Blue sharks often hunt in packs and circle their prey before attacking. Although these creatures normally eat fish and squid, they will attack humans.

▲ Great white sharks are fearsome predators. They have rows of ultra-sharp triangular teeth that are perfect for taking large bites out of prey, such as seals, sea lions and dolphins.

Grey reef sharks are sleek, swift predators of the Indian and Pacific oceans. Unusually, they give plenty of warning before they attack. If the grey reef shark feels threatened, it drops its fins down, raises its snout and starts weaving and rolling through the water.

Peril at the shore

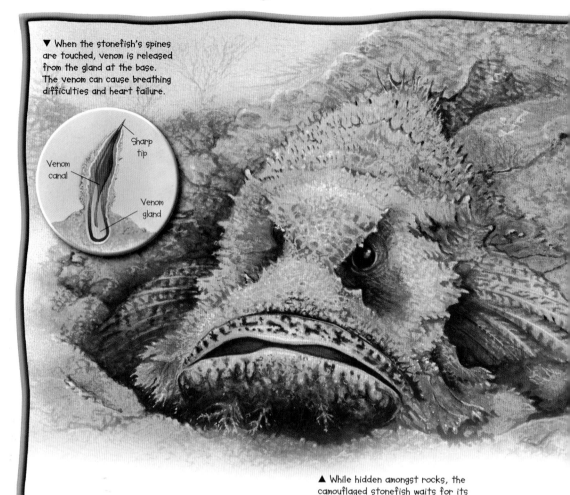

▼ When the stonefish's spines are touched, venom is released from the gland at the base. The venom can cause breathing difficulties and heart failure.

Sharp tip

Venom canal

Venom gland

▲ While hidden amongst rocks, the camouflaged stonefish waits for its prey, such as small fish.

The seashore may seem like a quiet place, but danger lies beneath the gently lapping waves. While some predators actively hunt their prey, some creatures just sit and wait.

Stonefish may look like a piece of rocky coral, but their cunning disguise hides a deadly surprise. One touch of the sharp spines on the stonefish's back results in an injection of venom, which may be fatal.

DESIGN TIME

You've now read about lots of dangerous animals and the tools they use to kill their prey. Now it's time to draw or paint your own deadly creature.

Will it have claws, fangs, spikes, venom or horns?

What will you call it? Perhaps a clawfish or a dragon monkey?

Sea snakes spend their lives in water. They breathe air, so they need to keep returning to the surface. All sea snakes are poisonous, and although their bites are painless at first, the venom is very powerful and can kill.

Lionfish are graceful swimmers, but the long spines on their fins inject venom as swiftly as a needle. A single injury from one spine causes immediate sickness and great pain, but it is unlikely to prove deadly to a human.

Seashells are not always as harmless as they appear. Rather than chasing their prey, cone shells attack other animals using a poison that paralyzes the victim so it cannot escape. The venom of fish-eating cone shells can paralyze a fish within seconds. Although their venom can be fatal to humans, it is being used by scientists to develop medicines that reduce pain.

▼ Cone shells use their long proboscis to shoot a poisonous dart into their prey. The venom is very powerful and quickly paralyzes the prey.

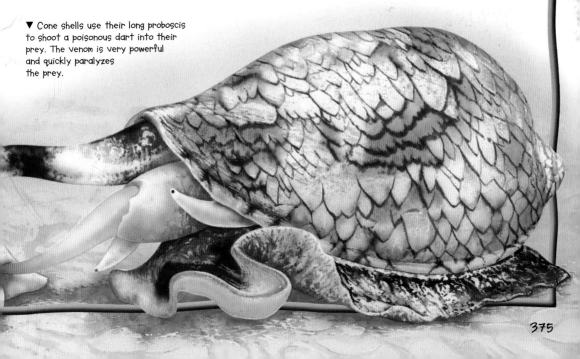

Minibeasts

◀ Although houseflies do not have stings, they are dangerous to humans. They can spread diseases if they land on food.

Animals don't have to be big to be beastly. There are many small animals, particularly insects, that are killers. Some of them, such as ants, are predators that hunt to eat. Others, such as locusts, cause destruction that affects humans.

Ants are found almost everywhere, except in water. Most ants are harmless to humans, but army ants and driver ants turn tropical forests and woodlands into battlefields. The stings of army ants contain chemicals that dissolve flesh. Once their prey has turned to liquid, the ants can begin to drink it.

▼ Millions of army ants live in a single group, or colony. They hunt together, swarming through leaf litter and attacking anything in their way.

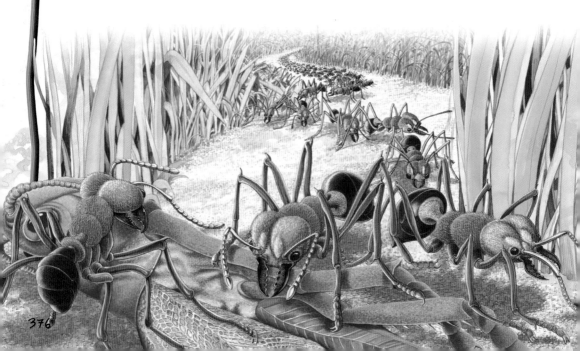

Driver ants have large jaws that can slice easily through food. They hunt in large numbers and swarm through forests hunting for prey. Driver ants can kill large animals, such as cows, by biting them to death. They have also been known to strip a chicken down to its skeleton in less than a day.

Deadly plagues of locusts have been written about for thousands of years. When they search for food, they travel in swarms of millions, eating all the plants they encounter. This can leave humans without any food.

▲ Killer bees fiercely protect their hive by swarming around it. They will attack anything that approaches the nest.

Killer bees are a new type of bee that was created by a scientist. He was hoping to breed bees that made lots of honey, but the bees proved to be extremely aggressive. Killer bees swarm in huge groups and when one bee stings, the others quickly join in. One sting is not deadly, but lots of bee stings can kill a human. It is thought that about 1000 people have been killed by these minibeasts.

Index

Index

Index

Index